Love's Philosophy

Love's Philosophy
Richard White

ROWMAN & LITTLEFIELD PUBLISHERS, INC.
Lanham • Boulder • New York • Oxford

ROWMAN & LITTLEFIELD PUBLISHERS, INC.
Published in the United States of America
by Rowman & Littlefield Publishers, Inc.
4720 Boston Way, Lanham, Maryland 20706
www.romanlittlefield.com

12 Hid's Copse Road
Cumnor Hill, Oxford OX2 9JJ, England

British Library Cataloguing in Publication Information available

Library of Congress Cataloging-in-Publication Data

White, Richard J. (Richard John), 1956–
  Love's philosophy / Richard White.
   p. cm.
  Includes bibliographical references (p.) and index.
  ISBN 0-7425-1256-8 (alk. paper) — ISBN 0-7425-1257-6 (pbk. : alk. paper)
  Love. I. Title.

BD436.W48 2001
128'.46—dc21   2001019747

The paper used in this publication meets the minimum requirements of American National Standard for Information Sciences—Permanence of Paper for Printed Library Materials, ANSI/NISO Z39.48-1992.

Nothing in the world is single:
All things by a law divine
In one spirit meet and mingle.
Why not I with thine?
—*Shelley, "Love's Philosophy" (1819)*

"Scholar," saieth Love, "Bend hitherward your wit."
—*Sir Philip Sydney, "Astrophel and Stella" (1591)*

Contents

Acknowledgments

Whatever else it may be, "the truth" is not a piece of private property that belongs to someone but to nobody else. And neither does the truth emerge fully formed from a single human brain without the interaction and involvement of others. Plato recognized this much when he used the dialogue form as the primary vehicle for his philosophical investigations. The dialogue is not the secondary and indifferent form to the true content of Plato's thought; rather, as Plato (or at least Socrates) understood, the truth is inherently dialogical in nature and can only emerge through conversation and discussion, or what he called "dialectic."

All of this is perhaps even more obvious when we turn specifically to the theme of love, for what we mean by "love" and our judgments about it depend almost completely on our experience of the world and our involvement with other people. Our understanding of what love is must emerge gradually through reading and discussion, dialogue, and living with other people. In this sense, every book is a joint production, and the author's name on a particular text can never represent "ownership" in any absolute sense.

Many people have played a part in the discussions and conversations that eventually led to the completion of this book. First, I would like to thank all of my colleagues in the Philosophy Department at Creighton University who have helped me and encouraged me in this project over the past few years. In particular, Patrick Murray, Jeanne Schuler, and Michael Brown all offered specific written suggestions on how to improve these chapters, and Peggy Troy helped very much with the final production of the text. I am also very grateful to my students in several Philosophy of

Love and Sex classes who challenged me to think clearly about love and who gave me direct and often brilliant advice on what is most important in these matters. Thanks to my son, Adam White, for putting up with this "labor of love" and for helping me to learn much about love in the process. My parents, Margaret and Jack White, have looked forward to this book for a long time: I am grateful to them; I am also grateful to Deborah Chaffin, who has helped and encouraged all of my writing over the years. Finally, I would like to thank Clarinda Karpov, who has given me so much to be thankful for. Her own ideas about love have significantly shaped my own, and the dialogue between us has inspired the following text. This book is for her.

Earlier versions of some sections of this book appeared in the following publications:
"Friendship: Ancient and Modern," *International Philosophical Quarterly* 39, no. 1 (March 1999): 19–34. Used by permission of the publisher.
"Friendship and Commitment," *Journal of Value Inquiry*, no. 33 (1999): 79–88. Used by permission of Kluwer Academic Publishers.
"The Future of Romantic Love," *International Studies in Philosophy*, 29, no. 2 (1997): 95–103. Used by permission of Scholars Press.

Introduction

A single word, love, is used to cover a variety of different experiences and relationships, including friendship and romance, altruism, and the caring of parents for their children. This might suggest that the ordinary concept of love is overburdened because it brings together things that are apparently quite different, and that when we talk about love in general we might be ignoring important distinctions that should be made. The Greeks, it is sometimes pointed out, had different words for each of the different kinds of love—including eros, philia, and agape—but they did not gather all of these experiences into a unitary concept. This may have been an oversight or just a feature of their language, or they may have been correct to maintain the ultimate differences between these related passions.

In any case, we can begin by noting that there is something problematic with the very idea of a "theory of love" that just assumes without question that there has to be a common core that underlies every specific manifestation of loving. This is a big assumption to make. The forms of friendship, romantic love, altruism, and parental love all have their own particular histories. The ancient Greeks would probably find the contemporary ideal of friendship somewhat limited and inadequate, and even within our own culture friendships between men often have a significantly different form than friendships between women or friendships between women and men. Of course, there may be a relationship of "family resemblance" between all of the different versions of friendship, but this is not the same as an underlying identity that would *itself* be based on the deeper principle of "love." And if we accept that

love has no empirical reality apart from the particular manifestations of friendship, romance, altruism, or parental love, then it follows that we can only understand love through a discussion of
these particular determinations. We should therefore be suspicious
of any a priori account that ignores or abstracts from the reality of
particular experiences to legislate the nature of love in advance.
Such an account may simply enshrine the author's own experience
of love or, in the interests of a timeless theory of loving, may ignore
the diversity of love's history and its cultural forms.

On the other hand, the discussion of love would also be limited
and impoverished if it remained entirely on the level of description
of particular experiences of love. Just to survey the different kinds
of love in no way clarifies our understanding of it. The fact is, we
do recognize different examples as instances of romantic love or
friendship; we can compare or contrast the experience of love in
one culture with the experience of love in another; and we can
identify better and worse examples of friendship or parental love,
which are not simply reflections of our own contemporary perspective. All of this suggests that a more authentic account of
"love" and its different forms could become explicit through
reflection and discussion of love's particular manifestations. Not
that we will ever reach a final and exact theoretical account (for
love is not a timeless scientific object); but in making sense of our
own experience and comparing it with other models that are available, we will be able to clarify the nature of love, at least in its most
important manifestations. And this will give us an evaluative ideal
that should help us to distinguish between authentic and deficient
forms of loving.

This philosophical account of love, or "love's philosophy," is
therefore directed toward the truth of love, insofar as it describes
and evaluates the different forms of love and projects the possibility of a future ideal. But in what respect can we sensibly talk about
the "truth" of love? To some extent or other, the different manifestations of love are suffused with images, myths, and ideals that
condition much of our thinking as well as our experience of love
itself. Romantic love, for example, is dominated by the myth of the
one and only—the idea that there is only one other person in the
world for me, and that when I meet that person I will somehow
just "know" it. Also, as in the case of Tristan and Isolde, it projects
the goal of a final fusion between two lovers that allows them to
participate in eternity within this world. According to all the popular songs and stories, romantic love represents the fulfillment of

individual existence, without which life would be wretched and miserable.

These are all myths that we live by. This does not mean that they must be false, but for the most part they remain unchallenged and taken for granted as the essential truth about romantic love. In other cultures and ages, romantic love has not possessed such a priority; it has sometimes been regarded as an aberration and a dangerous affair that called the social order into question. In the Middle Ages, the love between Lancelot and Guinevere was both celebrated and condemned because it ultimately led to civil war and the end of the Arthurian age. And at the very beginning of modern times, in one of the first romantic novels, *The Sorrows of Young Werther,* Goethe shows the romantic hero as someone who destroys the harmony of the decent household. Thus, any adequate account of love must pay attention to the ruling ideology of love that is to be found in literature, music, art, and film and that is then reflected in our own experience of the world. A full account of the different forms of love can therefore only be given once we also have a real understanding of the place of love within the total economy of a given culture. Romantic love is an experience of individual intensity and fulfillment, but it is also related, both historically and conceptually, to the rise of the individual and individualism at the end of the modern age. This is not to dismiss romantic love or to diminish its importance, but it should make us question whether romantic love, as it is commonly understood, is actually a timeless possibility of all human life.

Only after these ideals and expectations have been described can we begin a critical reflection in order to determine their consistency and their real value for the enhancement of human life. Philosophical reflection on love must involve an evaluation of contemporary ideas and feelings about love. In such an evaluation, different ideas and conceptions of love will be found to be inspiring or inadequate, repressive or enhancing for human life in general from the standpoint of some criterion such as "personal fulfillment." Thus, at a certain point we must decide whether the prevailing model of friendship is consistent and uplifting, or whether the model must be rejected because it is impossible or falls short of its own inherent ideal. The same is true for the figure of the "perfect mother" that we often associate with parental love, or the romantic ideal of total self-abandonment and devotion.

It should be clear, then, that a purely conceptual analysis of love would be inappropriate and inadequate since it would not be critically grounded in the ruling ideas about love that we have inherited from the past. To understand the forms of love in our own culture, we must have some awareness of the historical and conceptual genealogy of these ideas and the role they play in the overall functioning of society. But at the same time, a purely empirical approach that simply describes the variety of personal experiences and the history of love's forms would also fall short, for it is the philosophical reflection on these experiences and ideas that enables us to determine which of them are the most valid as opposed to those that are really only masks for other passions, including jealousy and the desire for possession and control.

In this work, I use both of these perspectives in order to grasp the deepest critical understanding of love, and I am sure that some commonalities between the different kinds of loving will emerge. This is not to say that "love" exists apart from these particular manifestations, but it is to understand a range of experiences of loving that are apparently related to each other without being sub-sumed by any overarching ideal of the form of love itself. There is no obvious place to begin these discussions, and no obvious place to end. But we can start in the very midst of things by considering a very popular idea about the nature of love to determine whether it can withstand critical reflection or must now be abandoned as inadequate.

It is sometimes said that love is an emotion that involves the cherishing and profound attachment to another person. This emotion can either be actual or latent. I do not have to be in a state of continual yearning in order to really love someone. Sometimes I may even be angry with my friend or lover, but when the beloved is unhappy or when our relationship is threatened, this will certainly evoke an emotional response on my part because when I love someone I care deeply about that person and about my attachment to him or her. In this respect, underlying love is a sense of wonder at the other person and a strong sense of that person's unique and irreplaceable identity. Romantic love dies whenever one of the parties loses this sense of wonder, or when the couple becomes completely habituated to each other. Likewise, a loving parent may be challenged and even overwhelmed by her defiant child, but when that child is finally sleeping, the parent can step back from all the turmoil of the day and be overcome with a sense of wonder at the child who is now resting and calm.

Such experiences are always possible with those whom we love because our love is sustained by wonder, and it is a sense of wonder concerning the beloved that first pulls us out of ourselves and puts us in touch with something that goes beyond all our ordinary projects and concerns—Plato will call it "eternal" and "divine." Love thus involves a very deep appreciation for the absolute value of the other person. In romantic love especially, the beloved is often idealized as one who can do no wrong. While in general, loving someone usually involves putting the best possible interpretation on all of the loved one's words and actions, for we want to see him or her in the best possible light. Similarly, to love someone involves taking that person seriously. If something is important to the beloved then it must also be important to me. To tell a friend that her concerns or goals are ridiculous is not a friendly act, for in loving a friend we cherish her as the subject of her own life, and her concerns and goals may become just as important to us as our own.

Love therefore involves a deeply felt emotion of cherishing another person. But while this much may be necessary, it is not clear that it is also sufficient. In Tolstoy's *Anna Karenina*, for example, there is a famous scene in which Levin is "stupefied with happiness" after Kitty tells him that she loves him. He is blissfully happy and projects this happiness onto everyone that he meets in an outpouring of universal love:

> Levin saw from this secretary's face what a good, nice, kindhearted person he was. This was evident from his confusion in reading the minutes. . . . Levin . . . saw clearly that these people were not at all angry but were all the nicest, kindest people, and everything was as happy and as charming as possible between them. They did no harm to anyone, and were all enjoying it. What struck Levin was that he could see through them all today, and from little, almost imperceptible signs he knew the soul of each, and saw distinctly that they were all good at heart.[1]

The problem is that such enthusiasm cannot last, and because it is more of a projection than a response to someone else, we should have to say that whatever else Levin is going through it is not love. He is not responding to others and delighting in their existence; he is actually ignoring the reality of the others and projecting his feelings onto them, so that what he encounters is really only a reflection of himself. A similar point is made by those who would distinguish authentic love from infatuation. We might fall madly in love with someone that we do not even know—a celebrity or someone that we've seen from afar but never spoken to or interacted with in any way. But on reflection one probably would not say that this form of attachment is any kind of love, for since we do not "know" the other person, and have no shared history with him or her, we are not responding to an actual person but only indirectly to ourselves through a projection of our own making.

Let us now add, then, that as well as a deeply felt emotional attachment to another person, love must also involve a responsive caring for that person and a general willingness to help and for the latter's well-being. Thus, I may have positive feelings for another person, but if I am not prepared to help him either physically or emotionally, then I cannot really call myself his friend. This suggests that love and knowledge must go together, for if I care for someone it means that I am ready to help that person, which implies sharing some kind of a personal history, that is, coming to know that person and determining what it is that he or she needs. Of course, this is not just a matter of responding to requests but more significantly it involves encouraging the other person and helping her to become her own better self.

In his moral philosophy, Kant explicitly distinguishes between these two aspects of love. According to him, "pathological" love for someone else is based on mere sentiment or feeling, and it is unstable and unreliable because it follows our own inclinations rather than the needs of the other person. On the other hand, "practical" love, the higher kind of love, is based on reason and is independent of our pathological response to another. "It is in this sense," he writes,

> that we should understand too the passages from Scripture in which we are commanded to love our neighbour and even our enemy. For love out of inclination cannot be commanded; but kindness done from duty—although no inclination impels us, and even although natural and unconquerable disinclination stands in our way—is practical, and not pathological, love, residing in the will, and not in the propensions of feeling, in principles of action and not of melting compassion; and it is this practical love alone which can be an object of command.[2]

As a parent, for example, I may not even like my children, and maybe there is nothing that I can do about that. But, Kant would say, I must show them practical love by caring and providing for them and raising them properly as parents are supposed to do. He may have a point here about what is most important for the child. And yet, we would probably wonder whether such a relationship could really count as "loving" at all. The ability to care for another person and to be responsive and available to him or her is an essential part of love, but without any kind of emotional attachment this would seem to be caretaking as opposed to caring and would not rise to the level of an authentic love. Hence, both the practical and pathological forms of love that Kant separates for the sake of analysis must be present in any example of authentic loving. These are really two different aspects of the same thing, and love would not be present if one were either unaffected by the other person or unavailable to her.

Now it would seem to be the case that there are no necessary objects of love, for we can love our friends, children, animals, and perhaps even inanimate objects such as cars. But there are different ways of relating to the beloved, and in what follows I argue that the most basic of these are friendship, romantic love, parental love, and altruism. Each of these entails a sense of relationship to the other and a corresponding enlargement of the self that follows thereby. I have already described how the beloved affects me by pulling me out of my everyday existence and putting me in touch with something that transfigures ordinary life. Now I will add that this is not just a passive relationship of contemplative wonder, for through my attachment to the beloved I experience an enlargement of my own sense of self. It is not only that the beloved matters but, more important, that the beloved matters to me, in the sense that when I love someone his or her joys and sorrows become my joys and sorrows too. I do not just feel sad for my child when she is unhappy; I also feel unhappy. And I am happy when my friend receives good news because my own emotional well-being is totally bound up with the well-being of all those whom I love.

In the case of altruism or humanitarian love, the same principle is at stake, for when I am affected by the plight of the stranger and feel compelled to help, I am responding to my own sense of connectedness to that person (and perhaps to everyone else in the world). He or she is another human being like me, and what happens to that person matters to me. More than just submitting to an abstract duty, such as the obligation to exercise charity, I am moved to help that person because I recognize that I have something in common with him or her. In this sense, love involves a personal transformation and emotional growth through the beloved. Likewise, to love someone means to make oneself vulnerable, for I am deeply affected by the misery, death, or desertion of the beloved. If I am totally unaffected by the one I claim to love—if, for example, I am that parent who raises his child in a decent way but who is not in any way challenged or transformed by him—then it is not clear that I do love that person, since loving requires an openness to the other and hence the possibility of transformation through the beloved.

There is another aspect to the dialectical relationship between the self and the other that loving involves. Traditionally, both in philosophy as well as in popular culture, a conflict has been held to exist between the ideal of autonomy and being with others, in the sense that being attracted and attached to others is viewed as a kind of self-abandonment that destroys one's own self-rule. Love is perceived as a wound in the armor of self-sufficiency, for the more I am drawn to others and take their needs and wishes to be just as important as mine, the more vulnerable I am to misery and loss. In the *Symposium*, for example, Alcibiades offers a portrait of Socrates as someone who is totally self-contained. Alcibiades is madly in love with Socrates and tries everything to get Socrates to fall for him. But Socrates remains aloof, and we are probably meant to admire Socrates's extreme self-sufficiency and his self-control, which cannot be deflected by the lure of physical beauty. In fact, in the *Symposium*, Socrates, through Diotima, describes the whole progression of love, from the love of individual beauty to love of all physical beauty, love of moral beauty, and love of principle, ending with the love of the good. But once this final point is reached, it seems that we would no longer need anything or anyone to enjoy this rapturous state. As Diotima argues:

> And if . . . man's life is ever worth the living, it is when he has attained this vision of the very soul of beauty. And once you have seen it, you will never be seduced again by the charm of gold, of dress, of comely boys, or lads just ripening to manhood; you will care nothing for the beauties that used to take your breath away and kindle such a longing in you . . . to be always at the side of the beloved and feasting your eyes upon him, so that you would be content, if it were possible, to deny yourself the grosser necessities of meat and drink, so long as you were with him.[3]

This is basically the condition that Socrates is in. His self-sufficiency has made him impervious to love. The corollary to this is the idea that romantic love involves such a complete devotion to the other person that it requires self-abandonment and the loss of one's own self-rule and subjection to another. In both cases, love and autonomy are viewed as mutually exclusive.

Following what I have already argued, however, this would seem to be one of those ruling ideas about love that must now be challenged. Certainly, as Freud recognized, love can serve as a front for self-abandonment, or for any other kind of passion for that matter, including the desire for possession and control. And in some love affairs, the more the beloved is exalted the more the lover feels emptied out and worthless. But set against this is the very real sense in which we can come to know and understand ourselves through loving another person. Through loving our children, our friends, our partners, and humanity in general we gain the strongest sense of who we are. And this is not surprising: Love is one of the most intense forms of relationship, and our sense of self, our sense of who we are, is largely formed in relation to other people, since it is in their responses of approval and disapproval, and in the consciousness of our responses to them, that we gain a mirror to ourselves. In this respect, Aristotle argued specifically that the friend is "another self." But as I show in this book, each kind of love inspires self-enlargement and self-understanding to some extent, and in this way love promotes individual autonomy rather than destroying it.

In short, love is a stimulus to personal transformation, and it can lead to self-knowledge and self-fulfillment as the most complete expression of who we are. This does not mean that love is self-regarding in any narrow sense. To love one's child, for example, entails an obvious expansion of concern—my child's happiness matters deeply to me. But at the same time, I want that child to be happy even if this must involve her separation from me. As a parent I expect that my children will grow up and leave one day, and while I hope that my relationship with them will continue to be strong, this is actually less important to me than their own flourishing as independent human beings. Thus, in general, we might say that in love my concern for another is really inseparable from my concern for myself. Likewise, it is a false abstraction to separate my own good from the good of the ones whom I love, since in love, my sense of belonging with another has become a fundamental aspect of who I am.

What emerges from the discussion so far is that the enquiry into love requires attention to three basic axes. First, there is the focus upon the other person, the reorientation of one's self in terms of his or her needs and desires, and the idealization of the beloved that usually occurs in love. Next, there is the enlargement of the self and the transformation of who we are, and who we think we are, that our relationship to the beloved brings about. Finally, going beyond both the self and other, or the two poles of this relationship, there is the relationship itself. Sometime I may have to choose between what is good for me in particular, or for the beloved, and what is good for our relationship itself. And so I might ask, does such a relationship need to be reciprocal? And does it have a natural trajectory of its own? The different axes I have described are not really separable from each other. They are three different moments of the same experience, but for the purpose of analysis it is useful to distinguish them from the outset. And I have emphasized, all of this needs to be understood in the context of the cultural and historical formations that have conditioned the ruling ideas about love.

In the following chapters, I examine the four basic kinds of love: friendship, romantic love, parental love, and the love of humanity. I consider the popular understanding of each kind of love as well as the inherent ideal to which it seems to aspire. In the case of friendship, for example, there is the sense today that to be friends, individuals must spend time together, enjoy each other's company, and share activities and interests. This suggests a side-by-side relationship with apparently little depth. But if we compare this to the Greek model of friendship, it becomes clear that the contemporary ideal fails to recognize the sense in which friendship is an inherently moral activity, which is what is most fulfilling in such a relationship. Through consideration of the facts of friendship and its purported ideal, another, more appropriate, model may then emerge for us that will help us to understand ourselves and the final significance of this particular kind of love. In the case of friendship, I dwell on this relationship between love and moral development.

Since the beginning of the modern age, romantic love has become a very popular and important ideal, and we are encouraged to believe that falling in love is all-important and that without romantic bliss life would be wretched and unfulfilled. We consequently experience great anxiety concerning our romantic lives, for we are encouraged to define ourselves by them. In looking at romantic love, however, I will describe the ways in which typically romantic speculations can lead to misery and a sense of failure. If the romantic model, as popularly understood, is too exalted or even impossible for most people, then we must revalue romantic love and think beyond its contemporary forms to a postromantic form of encounter that would enable the spiritual, emotional, and physical fulfillment of both women and men. In particular, we must try to articulate a new form of passionate love that would involve both autonomy and connectedness and that would honor both the spiritual and the physical sides of our nature. Presumably, this would also transcend the sexist appropriation of romantic love that has prevailed so far in Western culture.

In discussing the love of parents for their children, I focus on the forms of caring, which certainly exist in any loving relationship but seem to be most crucial in the case of parental love. There are some very powerful models in our culture for what it means to be a perfect mother or a good father. The former is characterized by softness and self-sacrifice, while the latter involves the strict assertion of law in all circumstances, even when one would like to relax or be merciful. The Virgin Mary is the paradigm of the first ideal, and Manlius, the Roman commander who executed his own son for disobeying orders, is an example of the second. Once again, the analysis may show that the whole intention and the implicit goal of parental love are inconsistent with these received ideas about what it means to be a loving parent, and so the guiding model of such a love may have to be reconstrued.

In the case of humanitarian love, or the love of humanity, I show how our love and caring for those who we do not even know cannot be based on either a selfish impulse or a purely altruistic one. Such love illuminates our deep connection with the rest of humanity and ultimately, perhaps, to the whole of nature and everything else that exists. People such as Oskar Schindler who rescued Jews during World War II were responding to this sense of connection and belonging to others. What moved them was not an irrational decision to help or a response to a moral duty, but a lived connection to others that they could not repudiate without in some sense repudiating themselves. In this respect, I suggest that the love of humanity both expresses and confirms our connection to all others in the ultimate order of things.

Such loves may never exist in their pure form, for friendship and romantic love may often be combined, and a parent may also be a friend to his children. But they are the most basic varieties of love, and together they can help us understand the total experience of loving. Every experience of love must involve at least one of these particular manifestations, and any conclusions about "love in general" can only come after these particular enquiries have been completed.

Likewise, it is also important to point out that there is no hierarchy here. I do not want to claim that friendship is inferior to romantic love or that the love of humanity is (as Kierkegaard argues) the fulfillment of love since it is the least selfish and the only kind of love that does not seem to depend on our own desires and wishes. On the contrary, each kind of love evokes and appeals to a different aspect of who we are. And in this sense, each is equally important as a key to the total understanding of what love is.

Finally, I have not chosen to include religious love or self-love in this discussion. Religious love is not really a distinct type of love, except in terms of its object, which is usually God. Thus, in a Christian context, some people will consider Jesus Christ as their savior and friend, while others, like Saint Theresa of Avila, will describe the religious experience in quasi-erotic or romantic terms. Others might say that God loves us unconditionally like a good parent. Still others would argue that God's love and the love of God are inseparable from the agape or love of neighbor that is proclaimed in the gospels. In each case, the relationship to God is presented as the fulfillment of a particular kind of love, but it does not introduce a new kind of love that can be distinguished from friendship, romantic love, altruism, or parental love as such. Similarly, self-love seems to be practically equivalent to self-acceptance or self-respect. And since the subject and object of this love are identical, self-love is not a dynamic relationship that involves self-transformation and growth. Self-love is only "love" in a derivative and secondary sense. It does not involve a relationship to an other who challenges, enhances, or fulfills my sense of who I am. But without an "other" in this radical sense—without mediation, in fact—it would be very difficult, if not impossible, to achieve any kind of a relationship with oneself.

The four chapters that follow are to some extent self-sufficient investigations into the nature of the four most basic kinds of love. I consider romantic love, friendship, parental love, and humanitarian love from a variety of different perspectives, including philosophy, psychology, history, and literature. Each of these loves has a historical genealogy and is subject to cultural transformations. Each of these loves demonstrates the relevance of a philosophical inquiry into the nature of love. I emphasize the relationship between love and personal fulfillment and the very possibility of an authentic relationship with another person. The entire inquiry clarifies the nature of "love's philosophy."

1

Friendship and the Good

The ideal of friendship had a privileged place in the ancient world. This is not to say that the Greeks and the Romans were necessarily any better at making or keeping friends than we are. Cicero complains that in the whole history of the world there have only been a handful of true friends, and it is said that even Aristotle used to lament the failure of friendship with "O my friends, there is no friend."[1] But it is to also the case that friendship was much more frequently discussed in classical antiquity. Friendship served as an explicit regulative ideal and as a focus for self-understanding. Aristotle is probably representative of many classical writers, if not of classical antiquity in general, insofar as he argues that without friends one would not be able to live a good and flourishing life. Later Stoics and Cynics were perplexed by the apparent conflict between a goal of sovereign self-sufficiency and the openness and availability that friendship entails. But, significantly, they usually sought to resolve this tension by arguing, like Seneca, that true friendship presupposes the condition of sovereignty. Thus friendship in its highest form, perhaps unlike other loves, could never be based on a lack or a need, but only on the most complete "abundance" and generosity of spirit. For these classical authors, true friendship that goes beyond mutual using testifies to the fulfillment of the human spirit and can never be viewed as a restriction or a confinement.

Of course, it is misleading to talk in such general terms about the "ancient" conception of friendship as if it were a unitary phenomenon. There are plenty of differences between Plato and Aristotle, or Cicero and Seneca, and the philosophical discussion of friendship may not always correspond to the direction of popular thinking. Likewise, one might ask whether "friendship" in the classical world was a *representative* ideal that described an ongoing possibility of human experience, or a *compensatory* ideal that emphasized a way of relating to others that was conspicuously absent.[2] In fact, it is only when we compare these classical authors with our own contemporary intuitions concerning the nature and value of friendship that we recognize something like a "classical" account of friendship that stands in some contrast to our own. I begin this reflection on friendship by noting three essential points of difference that may guide our discussion in what follows.

The first point to note is the decline of friendship as an ideal, if not also as a reality, in modern life. It has been frequently noted, for example, that until very recently modern philosophers had all but abandoned the theoretical discussion of friendship. In the *Nicomachean Ethics*, Aristotle devotes two of ten books to friendship, which suggests its significance for living a good life. But apart from some brief but important essays by Montaigne, Bacon, Emerson, and others, there really has not been an original and sustained account of friendship in modern thought. Likewise, if we look directly at the preoccupations of modern life, it simply is the case that friendship is no longer the exalted ideal that it once was. What concerns us, I think, at least since the beginning of modern times, is the imperative of romantic love and the need to find someone with whom we might share the bliss of romantic union and the pleasures of domestic partnership. This preoccupation with and elevation of romantic love makes friendship something secondary. Thus we even say that someone is "just" a friend, which implies that as far as we are concerned, friendship is not the highest relationship of which we are capable.

The second point of contrast concerns the essentially moral aspect of friendship that the ancients seemed to insist on. If friendship is an apprenticeship in virtue, or a way of building character, then of course it would be impossible for a really bad person to be a good friend, even to another bad person. If Aristotle is right, then friendships based on pleasure or utility are certainly possible, but they are all deficient modes of friendship because the final tendency of friendship is toward virtue and the good. In response to this, one would have to say that from a contemporary perspective friendship is not obviously about virtue at all. We choose our friends on the basis of what we have in common and whether we enjoy being with them. Our friends *may* inspire us to become better people, but this will not always be the case. And even if we often do think of our friends as decent people, it is not clear that we have to. I may like someone and continue to think of her as a friend although I am well aware of all her moral failings. If it is said that such a relationship cannot be considered a *real* friendship, then this would only be a stipulative assertion, based on an a priori definition of what friendship is. In fact, we might say that from a contemporary perspective, to describe two people as "friends" does not entail anything about their moral involvement with each other.

Finally, it can be argued that the ancient conception of friendship enshrined by Aristotle, Cicero, and others is a very limited and ideologically burdened account. In the classical tradition the basic model of friendship that every commentator relies on is the ideal relationship between two (freeborn) adult males. In Plato's *Lysis,* the discussion takes place within an all-male setting, and Aristotle scarcely mentions the possibility of friendship between women except to suggest that the difference between male and female friendship is the difference between "the better person" and the worse. Cicero's examples of great friends are exclusively male. This view has certainly helped to create a bias in our own tradition that has often seen friendship as the exclusive achievement of men; but in recent years, this bias has been recognized and condemned.

The classical conception of friendship is elaborated within the total context of specific ideals that include autonomy, self-mastery, and the desire not to rely on others. As I have said, this leads to an abiding anxiety that friendship must be reconcilable with self-sufficiency; and the implicit endorsement of this (male) view of subjectivity leads to a gendered account of friendship. Aristotle and Cicero both insist, for example, that a good friend will avoid burdening his friends with his own troubles and pains. According to Aristotle, "That is why someone with a manly nature tries to prevent his friend from sharing his pain. Unless he is unusually immune to pain, he cannot endure pain coming to his friends; and he does not allow others to share his mourning at all, since he is not prone to mourn himself either." And he concludes, "Females, however, and effeminate men enjoy having people wail with them; they love them as friends who share their distress. But in everything we clearly must imitate the better person."[3]

Later, Seneca goes so far as to claim that the wise man does not need friends, and that he bears the loss of his friends with equanimity.[4] Such a claim is disconcerting because one suspects that this preoccupation with calm and detachment also involves the avoidance of any identification with the joys and sorrows of the other that we would characterize as friendship. Today, we might think that the willingness to appear vulnerable and open and the desire not to keep our emotional life to ourselves are essential ingredients of friendship, since friendship is a condition of mutual trust and availability to the other. I tell my friend about my fears and anxieties, as well as my achievements and strengths. But the classical conception of friendship is bound to downplay any emphasis on intimacy and the sharing of one's deepest concerns with the other person as an erosion of personal sovereignty and a consequent sign of weakness. Hence the classical account of friendship is male oriented and specifically aristocratic in tone. There is reason to believe that our contemporary understanding of friendship is informed by a very different context of values and ideals, and this must call into question the enduring validity of the ancient model. At the same time, however, we must acknowledge that many of the features of our own conception of friendship may also be ideologically driven.

What, then, is friendship? And if ancient and contemporary ideas about friendship are quite different, do we have any right to postulate a single concept that could then be analyzed and evaluated? Should we not say that friendship is an inherently complex and multiple phenomenon, so that to grasp the significance of friendship we would have to consider men's friendship, women's friendship, friendship in the ancient world and friendship between children, erotic friendship and Platonic friendship, to name but a few? Clearly, we must proceed with caution, and we should remain aware of two dangers in particular. First, we must avoid simply legislating the nature of friendship in the absence of any empirical support. There is, I believe, a core meaning or a set of meanings constitutive of "friendship." These can be recognized in the various manifestations of friendship, and indeed, they allow us to recognize these manifestations as examples of friendship in the first place. The contemporary and the ancient models of friendship are quite different, but they also have many points of similarity, which means that the comparison of the two will be mutually illuminating. Perhaps we cannot articulate the nature of friendship in any great detail, but it is to be hoped that we all have had the lived experience of friendship; we all have some intuitive understanding of friendship that usually allows us to recognize immediately when a friendship has been betrayed or when someone is not a good friend.

We must now try to make this lived experience of friendship more explicit. But at the same time—and this is the second danger—the discussion of friendship cannot be merely empirical or value free. The account of friendship that emerges in the following pages must be critical and self-questioning. We cannot construct a theory of friendship just by looking at the surveys and sociological reports that are based on what people actually think about their friends. Such an uncritical account would only enshrine the prevailing prejudices and make every other culture's understanding of friendship irrelevant to our own. Friendship is a value and an ideal that may or may not be given in daily life. Only the critical discussion of the established forms of friendship can help to clarify the authentic meaning of friendship, which may turn out not to exist for us.

In the following discussion, I will return to the points of conflict briefly outlined earlier. In the main part of this chapter I look at the essential differences between the ancient and contemporary conceptions of friendship, specifically, the ways in which Aristotle's account appears partial and limited when it is referred to as a model for today. Next, I consider how the Aristotelian account may provide us with a critique of contemporary friendship by emphasizing the ways in which friendship should still be viewed as a moral phenomenon and as a source of moral growth. Finally, in a more speculative conclusion, I consider the value and the significance of friendship within the total context of modern life.

Friendship: Ancient and Modern

At the very beginning of Book VIII of the *Nicomachean Ethics*, Aristotle argues that no one would ever choose to live without friends, even if he had all other goods. This is, I think, a true claim—it may even be obvious—but it is at the same time a profound and significant truth about human beings. Later, Aristotle explains, "Surely, it is absurd to make the blessed person solitary. For no one would choose to have all [other] goods and yet be alone, since a human being is political, tending by nature to live together with others" [1169b]. This suggests that being with others, and especially with those to whom we are friends, is not merely a desirable benefit of being alive but a fundamental condition for living a fully human existence and for appreciating the value of life in the first place.

Aristotle's philosophical account of friendship has remained the paradigm of friendship for those who succeeded him. And even though there has always been an enormous amount of scholarly controversy concerning the proper interpretation of his most basic ideas, Aristotle's account is in a real sense "definitive" for Cicero and other Roman writers who repeat many of Aristotle's themes and images, and also for St. Thomas Aquinas, whose discussions of love and friendship invariably follow Aristotle's lead. In fact, Aristotle's account of friendship remains influential and compelling, and for better or for worse it will continue to shape our own understanding of what exactly friendship is. At this point, then, we may briefly consider some of the main lines of Aristotle's argument and use this as a springboard for further discussion. It is clear that the conceptual landscape of Aristotle's philosophy is very different from our own, and he surely had a different understanding of the self and its relation to others that might explain some of the apparent difficulties of his account of friendship. But to the extent that the Aristotelian (and ancient) model of friendship is still relevant and still speaks to us, it must provide some direction for our own understanding of what it means to be a friend, and this emerges more or less directly from the text.

Aristotle, then, as is well known, distinguishes between three different kinds of friendship. The two lower forms are friendship that is based on utility and mutual need, and friendship that is based on pleasure and mutual enjoyment. Both of these forms of friendship are limited, however, because they only relate to a partial aspect of the other person. According to Aristotle, utility friendships will flourish only for as long as the friends remain useful to each other, while pleasure friendships are based largely on the impulse of youth and physical attractiveness, and so it is not in their nature to be enduring. In fact, Aristotle argues that only the "complete friendship" of virtue is friendship in the fullest sense, and as such it will be enduring for as long as the friends are good. "On this view," he writes, "the friendship of good people in so far as they are good is friendship in the primary way, and to the full extent; and the others are friendship by similarity" [1157a]. Of course, it is understood that any given friendship may include all three of the modalities that Aristotle describes—if my good (virtuous) friend helps me to find a job, then our friendship is useful to me at the same time as it helps me to become a better person. But the main point here is that what is most essential and valuable in such a relationship is its tendency to promote the life of virtue and hence the flourishing of the individuals involved.

In several places, Aristotle says that the friend is "another self," and this, I think, really emphasizes the respect in which friendship is a form of solidarity with those who are somehow "like" oneself.[5] In this way friendship promotes self-affirmation and encourages self-esteem. As "a second self," my friend is one who shares my own worldview and basic set of values. We will enjoy doing the same things together, and as we each find our own perspective and our own essential nature confirmed and endorsed by the other, we will gain a much stronger sense of our own self-worth. Similarly, by having friends we are able to achieve a real measure of self-knowledge, in the sense of "knowing who we are." My friend, as Cicero repeats, is a model of myself.[6] He or she provides the context of acceptance and trust that allows me to be myself without always seeking to please or impress. In such a relationship I can experience the contours of my own essential nature insofar as they affect or engage my friend. Presumably, this is why Aristotle affirms that friendship is an essential aspect of living the good life, for as solitary creatures we could never achieve a sense of who or what we are. It would be much harder, if not impossible, to affirm the value of our lives if we were totally cut off from others or could only relate to them in an impersonal and nonintimate way, for without the intimate connections of love and friendship our inner beings, as opposed to our public personas, would forever remain out of play.

Friendship is thus the most important arena for self-knowledge and continuing moral growth. And in *complete* friendship all of these tendencies are realized. As Aristotle explains:

> Complete friendship is the friendship of good people similar in virtue; for they wish goods in the same way to each other in so far as they are good, and they are good in themselves. [Hence they wish goods to each other for each other's own sake.] Now those who wish goods to their friend for the friend's own sake are friends most of all; for they have this attitude because of the friend himself, not coincidentally. Hence these people's friendship lasts as long as they are good; and virtue is enduring. [1156b]

An example of such a complete form of friendship might be the relationship between Jane Eyre and Mr. Rochester in Charlotte Brontë's novel. Although this is a romantic relationship that leads finally to marriage, Jane is at the same time portrayed as a real friend to Rochester, not just because she is dedicated to him and volunteers to look after him after he is crippled, but because she does all she can to restore his own self-reliance and self-esteem and is never afraid to challenge him when he acts selfishly or neglects the needs of others. Likewise, Rochester is drawn to her quiet but indomitable spirit and her deep moral sense that led her to leave him, in spite of her love for him, after their first abortive marriage ceremony. By the end of the novel, one has a strong sense of two people who completely respect and admire each other and who will devote themselves to cultivating the good that lies both within and between themselves. Their relationship is not based simply on physical attraction or mutual utility, like Rochester's relationship to Blanche Ingram, the local heiress. In fact, it is based on a third thing—virtue—that transcends the two individuals involved and provides the horizon for their involvement with each other.

Thus, true friendship—or complete friendship—cannot be selfish or self-regarding. In contrast to utility friendship, for example, it can never involve using the other person as a means to one's own happiness, and this means that it is not a relationship that involves only a very limited aspect of the other person. "And so those who love for utility or pleasure," Aristotle comments, "are fond of a friend because of what is good or pleasant for themselves, not in so far as the beloved is who he is, but in so far as he is useful or pleasant" [1156a]. By contrast, then, we would say that in complete friendship I am concerned with the happiness and well-being of another for his or her *own* sake, and not merely with regard to how this will affect me.

Regardless of whether one has read Aristotle before, this account of complete friendship is a familiar one, for Aristotle is only reminding us that in the most genuine forms of love all our joys and sorrows are completely commingled with the joys and sorrows of those who we care about most deeply. Thus I am not simply sad *for* my friend when he suffers a terrible disappointment, for this would mean that there is still a real distance between us. Nor by imagining how badly he must feel am I simply empathizing by imagining how this would feel to me. Instead I will tend to experience my friend's most significant disappointments and joys directly, as if they were my own, because of the emotional identification and enlargement of personal concern that true friendship, as a form of love, must always entail.

In this respect, then, it may be argued that in true friendship I am genuinely concerned with my friend's well-being as an end in itself, and in this sense, as Aristotle says, a friend *is* "another self." The problem, however, which has been pointed out before, is that such a complete friendship also suggests a devotion and concern for the other person that is basically unconditional. For if love, in general, involves an imaginative identification with the life of another, then should we not have to avoid making any negative judgments or complaints about our friends that imply that our love has its limits after all? The most obvious model for unconditional love is that of a parent for his or her child, since it is more than likely that no matter what that child does or how she turns out, the parent will continue to love her, and feel with her, even if the particular forms of that love may sometimes be experienced as oppressive. Aristotle, however, wants to link complete friendship to virtue. He does not mean to argue that such friendship is only possible between two moral saints. Complete friendship is the ideal mode that we should strive to incorporate in our dealings with friends as specific others who we care about. But if complete friendship is based on a mutual recognition and association in virtue, then it apparently follows that even in complete friendship my love and concern for my friend is not unconditional since it depends on his or her continuing goodness. Aristotle even asserts that if a good friend becomes bad we should conclude the relationship and drop him as a friend: "However, the friend who dissolves the friendship seems to be doing nothing absurd. For he was not the friend of a person of this sort; hence, if the person has altered, and he cannot save him, he leaves him" [1165b]. The question that emerges from this discussion is whether friendship really is based on an absolute concern for my friend as an unconditional end or whether friendship is, on the contrary, just another (albeit higher) manifestation of self-concern that only accepts the friend in a conditional sense.

Perplexingly enough, Aristotle himself seems to argue for the latter position when, in the fourth chapter of Book IX, he shows how the defining features of friendship toward one's neighbors may be derived from "features of friendship towards oneself." Thus a friend is said to be "someone who wishes and does goods or apparent goods to his friend for the friend's own sake" and who "wishes the friend to be and to live for the friend's own sake"; likewise, a friend is someone "who spends time with his friend," who "makes the same choices," and "who shares his friend's distress and enjoyment." But then Aristotle goes on to explain that the good man *also* wishes and does apparent goods *to himself,* he wants himself to live and be preserved, he spends time in his own company, and so forth. Thus, as some commentators have put it, Aristotle seems to derive altruism from egoism, insofar as he argues that the most important features of our friendship toward others are ultimately based on and even seem to follow from our own self-regarding concerns. Because the decent person has each of these features in relation to himself, Aristotle is able to conclude that he is "related to his friend as he is to himself, since the friend is another himself" [1166a].

Now, there is of course a sense in which it is a part of the popular wisdom that you cannot really love anyone else unless you have learned to esteem and value yourself. Many romantic relationships fail because the two partners expect, albeit unconsciously, that the relationship will solve all of their personal problems; but this is just a way of deferring the painful work that self-examination and acceptance requires. Hence, it does seem correct to say that in order to be a good friend to others one must already be a good friend to oneself. Likewise, we may also be prejudicing the issue by describing the way in which Aristotle derives "altruism" from "egoism." As Charles Kahn points out, these modern terms had no real equivalent for the Greeks.[7] This is *not* how we should think of what Aristotle is doing here, for in fact, in the same chapter, Aristotle distinguishes between two forms of self-love. On the one hand, whoever indulges the lower part of his nature is a "self-lover" in the bad sense called "selfish" and is justifiably reproached. On the other hand, the "self-lover" in a good sense is someone who is continually trying to gratify "the most controlling part of himself," that is, his *nous* or reason, and as such, Aristotle continues, he cannot be blameworthy for wanting to become a better person. Thus, a friend is *not* a self-lover in the common sense, and friendship is really *not* a self-regarding relationship that we only enter into insofar as it is in our own best interest.

And yet, these responses are not altogether satisfying. Even if we can separate a good from a bad form of self-love, it is still the case that this seems to make friendship into an exalted form of self-love. I am not convinced that this is helpful or correct; more immediately, however, it goes against the claim that friendship involves loving and caring for another for his or her own sake. Earlier, I described some of the benefits of complete friendship, including self-understanding, self-affirmation, individual moral development, and enhanced self-esteem. But while these are all good things, they are all good things *for me*, and if my friend benefits from these things it is only incidentally and not directly. Can Aristotle really be saying that our love and friendship for another is finally to be justified as an indirect way of achieving a higher self-regard? If so, friendship is *not* finally about loving another person as an end in himself or herself.

One famous example in the *Nicomachean Ethics* might actually confirm this: We are asked whether there can be any limit to the good things that we would wish for our friends, and Aristotle asserts that no one could ever wish that their friend would become a god, for while this is the greatest possible blessing it would also entail the end of the friendship since the gods are unconcerned with human affairs. This suggests, once again, the self-regarding bias of Aristotle's account, and the conditional nature of our commitment to our friends. In response, I suggest that while it is very useful to think of the friend as "another *self*," Aristotle (and, I think, most of the ancient commentators on friendship) loses sight of the fact that the friend is *another* self; rather than being ignored or rejected, it is precisely the "otherness" of the friend, within the context of sharing and similarity, that gives friendship its essential significance.

Now it must be said that for several commentators, the apparent difficulties in Aristotle's account of the friend as an end in himself are not insuperable. Both Kahn and Stern-Gillett, for example, have argued that Aristotle does not have a sense of the individual self as a being that is separate and self-contained.[8] This is a modern conception, and so are all of the puzzles regarding egoism and altruism that arise from it. For Aristotle, it is claimed, the individual self is largely identified with its controlling principle—with its *nous*, or reason—which is something that we share with all human beings. Thus two friends of outstanding character "will recognize in their common humanity and common rationality a unifying principle that makes their concern for one another possible, and which Aristotle's theory seeks to articulate."[9] From this perspective, I would not have to insist upon my "own" good because I would recognize my "own" good as something transpersonal that I share with everyone else. Indeed, this would be an ingenious resolution, since it would follow that if someone is bad, or incapable of self-control, then insofar as he is lacking a proper governing principle he is also lacking a self (in the deepest sense). Hence, it would no longer be possible to relate to this individual as a self-determining end in himself, and one could end the friendship without having violated the imperative that requires us to seek the well-being of our friends for their own sakes.

This solution does not really advance our understanding of the meaning of friendship, however. The recognition of our shared participation in virtue would give us, at best, a sense of solidarity and community, but as such an abstract concept, it does not explain the reality of friendship as a lived experience between individuals who enjoy and appreciate their own *differences* in perspectives and ideas. In this case, however, it is not Kahn and the other commentators who are to blame. In fact, Aristotle's whole account of friendship emphasizes solidarity and community and a shared vision of the common good. This is the stuff that binds individuals together at every level of society, including the interpersonal domain of friendship. What is missing, or at least underplayed, in Aristotle's account is the element of difference. This element becomes even more crucial when we are trying to figure out the place of friendship in our own modern life. Today, we no longer have a sense of the "common good" that is unanimously agreed upon; in fact, our society endorses a plurality of different and often competing goods, and we cannot presuppose a common framework of beliefs that must bind relationships together at every level. Today, perhaps, we also have a much stronger sense of "the individual" and the idea that every individual is unique and unrepeatable, and hence valuable in herself. We like to think that we are all different, whereas for the ancients, all of the individual heroes, such as Hector, Ajax, and Achilles, or the later sages, philosophers, and wise men, are basically "types." Thus, from the perspective of the highest good—whether this is *nous*, Athens, or Stoic reason—everything that is different or specific to a particular individual is actually irrelevant.

A part of the problem here lies in the translation of Aristotle from Greek to English. In English translations of Aristotle, the words *friend* and *friendship* are used as equivalents to Aristotle's *philos* and *philia*. What we need to remember, though, is that while this is really the only possible translation, the word *philia* literally refers to one's "nearest and dearest." Hence, in the *Nicomachean Ethics*, Aristotle refers to the relationship between husband and wife or parent and child, as well as that of two peers, as examples of *philia*. This is significant, because it means that what we might take to be one of the most essential aspects of peer friendship, namely, the fact that it is a voluntary and chosen relationship, is not emphasized in Aristotle, insofar as it is considered along with other familial and civic relations that we are not able to choose. It may seem obvious to us that, within certain limits, we *choose* who our friends are. For better or for worse, we were born into a given family as the citizen of a given country, but in choosing which relationships to cultivate as friendships, we are at the same time choosing and reconstituting ourselves. In friendship we are not given a community; rather, we create one, and our friends help us develop our own sense of who we are, insofar as they reflect back to us our own values and endorse the choices that we have made.

Friendship, then, in opposition to family and class, is a strong expression of individual values and self-determination. To a very great extent, we become who we are through our friendships. But this aspect is minimized in Aristotle, who emphasizes the *solidarity* of shared values and a common good to explain friendship as an inevitable expression at the local level of an ethos that permeates the whole of society. Significantly, for example, Aristotle spends some time explaining how in every community there is some sort of justice and a corresponding form of friendship. He argues that all of these communities are in fact subordinate to the political community—whether kingship, aristocracy, or timocracy—which implies that the forms of individual friendship are fully circumscribed and conditioned by the city itself.[10] Or, to put this another way, it is the public relationship between fellow citizens who are working together for the public good that serves as his model for interpersonal encounters. But while this may explain camaraderie and public spirit by emphasizing what people have in common, it does not explain individual friendships, which are intimate and private and not merely public affairs.

What, then, is most important about friendship? How does having friends help us? And is there a way of answering this question that does not commit us to "egoism" at either the higher or the lower level? In fact, friendship may bring all kinds of practical advantages and help, but these are secondary things and follow from the friendship itself. What is more basic here is that friendship involves caring about the well-being of another person, and cherishing this as an end in itself. This involves a more or less profound knowledge of who these friends are and an awareness of what they seek and value, as well as a willingness to reflect on oneself and to overcome any inner obstacles that may prevent one from accepting them and relating to them in an ongoing way.[11] For example, a man cannot be a good friend to a particular woman if he continues to have unthinking attitudes about "all women" and their place in life. Neither can a friendship develop between two people if they are absolutely unwilling to challenge their own perspectives and moral beliefs, for being a friend involves having a commitment to another person, and this means taking his or her perspectives and moral beliefs as seriously as one's own.

What all of this confirms, I think, is that like all other examples of genuine love, friendship involves the experience of positive recognition by an other, which is largely constitutive of personal selfhood and its moral limits vis-à-vis the world. But this recognition can only be given in a shared context of mutual concern—as Aristotle says, friendship has to be reciprocal—for one will experience the most positive and meaningful recognition from another person to the extent that one offers another the same recognition and appreciation that one's involvement in a friendship implies. The adulation of a slave or a fanatic is irrelevant to me. But within the sustained context of a friendship in which one's inner life is explored, recognition is absolutely meaningful because it comes from someone whom I regard as worthy of particular recognition myself. Thus friendship in its best form is the very opposite of a master-slave relationship because it is premised on the possibility of sharing, mutual disclosure, and vulnerability, and it only lasts for as long as these things are possible. If one friend is very open and reveals important desires and fears while the other simply does not reciprocate—which in this case would mean not to offer recognition—then the friendship will weaken or die, because the first friend will come to realize that the second friend is not prepared to take the same risk and to commit to another person in the way that he or she has.

From this very general account, then, we can now specify some of the essential features of friendship as a relationship that is grounded on recognition. The first is *equality*. Aristotle is right to argue that the further apart two people are in virtue, age, education, or in all the differences that make a difference, the more difficult it is to sustain a friendship. Hierarchical relationships such as those of parents and children do not foster real friendship because one party (in this case, the parent) seems to have most of the power and the ability to enforce his or her own perspective and rules whether or not the other party is in agreement. It is possible, however, that as children grow up they will become friends with their parents as their relationship becomes based on a more equal footing. Aristotle denied that a human being could ever become a friend to a god, and one suspects that in the Christian tradition all talk about Jesus being "my friend" must be figuratively or metaphorically intended, since in this case the distance between the benefactor and the beneficiary is held to be tremendous.

Second, and closely related to equality, is *reciprocity*. As I have said, friendship and recognition presuppose a lived engagement between two people who each value each other, and in being valued by the other, they are being valued by the one they respect and value beyond most others. Some forms of love do not require reciprocity—romantic love or parental love, for instance—but for two people to be friends they must both like each other and be open and available to each other. Reciprocity implies an ongoing dynamic of caring between two individuals who cherish and sustain each other. In effect, their friendship involves an implicit commitment to each other as people, and not merely to the values and principles that each party may espouse. Thus, it is possible for friends who share a similar outlook on life to have conflicts and disagreements, which they will overcome because they value each other as friends just as much as they value their own principles and commitments. Reciprocity involves taking the other person seriously, which means staying open and taking the other person's perspectives and commitments seriously too. Indeed, if friendship were not reciprocal in this sense, then it simply would not be a lived relationship with another person; it would be static, and recognition would be empty.

Third, and here again Aristotle is correct, friendship implies *solidarity*, or a basic sharing of values and perspectives and a similar sense of what is important and what is worth doing. People from different cultures will find it very difficult to make real friends with people outside of their own, and there is still a dispute, often reflected in the popular media, as to whether men and women can really be friends with each other, since they seem to have such different ways of thinking about life and relating to others. We must, I think, assume a shared horizon of concern, though not necessarily one of virtue, that relates people to each other to begin with. This is the common ground that Aristotle thought must unite all Athenian citizens with each other. Alternatively, it could be fellowship in Christ, which is supposed to cut across all external differences between believers to unite them as comrades in a common cause. As we have seen, Aristotle rightly emphasizes how friendship with another who is somehow *like* oneself provides us with a relevant image of ourselves and what it is that we really value. Likewise, he points out that the *shared* horizon of friendship encourages one to continue valuing a way of life or a set of commitments that one would find much harder to sustain by oneself.

Finally, however, and in obvious dialectical tension with solidarity, it is also important to recognize *alterity* as an essential aspect of friendship, which involves the recognition of the other as separate and different from us. Perhaps with other forms of love, and especially romantic love, the goal is some kind of merging with the other person in the bliss of mutual abandonment. But this is not the case with friendship, in which the specific difference of the other person's individual history and thinking about the world remains absolutely important. As I have argued earlier, friendship, like all other forms of love, involves an enlargement of being and my own sense of personal concern by incorporating my friend's fears and desires as if they were my own. But at the same time, it must also be said that friendship depends on the difference of the other person, which must be maintained in order for genuine recognition to take place. Thus, hoping that my friend fares well usually implies that I want my friend to have whatever she has decided that she must have in order to flourish. I may have no interest in medieval philosophy, but if my friend is absolutely enthralled with medieval philosophy and has applied for a place at a university, then I will naturally want her to be accepted so that she can study what she loves. This is in contrast to parental love, for even though we love our children, we do not always want them to have what they want for themselves. An ambitious industrialist may love his son very much, but this does not mean that he would support his son's desire to study medieval philosophy if it kept him from joining the family business. Friendship, however, involves respecting the other for her own sake, which means affirming and celebrating that individual for what she is and desires, without any attempt to shape or control her. Of course, this will lead on occasion to disagreement and even conflict with our friends, but it is the ability to work with this tension and to use it as a means for personal growth that characterizes friendship as a dynamic form. We hope that our best friends *will* challenge us and force us to become better than we are. And this provocation to virtue depends on respecting and even valuing the difference between us.

If the essence of friendship is connected to recognition, as I have argued here, then it follows that these four conditions—equality, reciprocity, solidarity, and alterity—must be regarded as the essential conditions for recognition that must therefore be present in order for friendship to exist. Aristotle's account of friendship apparently falls short because it does not really consider alterity, while it emphasizes all of those things that citizens would share in common. Today we would be much more likely to emphasize our differences, whereas what we share would be harder to discern. Let us now consider some of the consequences of this apparent shift in perspective, and how the recognition of a real difference between ancient and modern perspectives must lead us to challenge the validity of the ancient model and to reevaluate our contemporary philosophical understanding of what friendship is.

In his book *After Virtue*, Alasdair MacIntyre has also written about the difference between the ancient and the modern conception of friendship, but his reading assumes the primacy of the ancient (Aristotelian) formulation, which he uses as a measure to see how far we have fallen:

> This notion of the political community as a common project is alien to the modern individualist world. This is how we sometimes at least think of schools, hospitals or philanthropic organizations; but we have no conception of such a form of community concerned, as Aristotle says the *polis* is concerned, with the whole of life, not with this or that good, but with man's good as such. It is no wonder that friendship has been relegated to private life and thereby weakened in comparison to what it once was.
>
> Friendship of course, on Aristotle's view, involves affection. But that affection arises within a relationship defined in terms of a common allegiance to and a common pursuit of goods. The affection is secondary, which is not in the least to say unimportant. In a modern perspective affection is often the central issue; our friends are said to be those whom we *like*, perhaps whom we like very much. "Friendship" has become for the most part the name of a type of emotional state rather than a type of social or political relationship.[12]

This is an interesting comment for what it reveals about the author's own point of view. In this passage, MacIntyre makes a strict distinction between friendship as a part of social and political life (the part that Aristotle insists on) and friendship as a mere emotional state or a matter of liking. But such an opposition is deeply problematic insofar as it asserts, without any argument, the peripheral and secondary character of private life and the life of the emotions. It also assumes that the emotions are "unreasonable" and that private life is inherently nonpolitical. We should be suspicious of such emphatic oppositions, and we must consider what might be lost in our thinking about friendship if we continue to regard emotional involvement and fulfillment as a secondary concern. Indeed, it may be argued from a feminist perspective that the deep involvement with another person that constitutes friendship is only possible through the intimacy and emotional disclosure to the other that expresses a giving of oneself.[13] Of course, this runs counter to the traditional (male) version of friendship that has usually been upheld as the only model of friendship. Intimacy and emotional involvement are typically understood as "female" qualities and therefore, as in MacIntyre's passage above, they have frequently been rejected as secondary aspects of friendship itself.

Another example may clarify this point. In the 1950s, C. S. Lewis discussed friendship and other forms of love in a series of radio broadcasts that eventually became *The Four Loves*. In many respects, what Lewis has to say about friendship is interesting and sympathetic, and he is not usually dogmatic. But at the same time, his whole discussion reflects the same male paradigm of friendship that Aristotle endorsed. At one point, for example, Lewis says that friends (in the strong sense) never talk about their friendship. It is just accepted that the friendship is there, and so, in opposition to romantic love, it needs no discussion or commentary.[14] Likewise, he claims that friends, as opposed to lovers, hardly ever talk about each other and the intimacies of their own lives. He draws a portrait of two friends in a comfortable side-by-side relationship that is completely opposed to the intense face-to-face encounter that is supposed to characterize romantic love. In fact, according to Lewis it is obvious that "friends don't want to know each others' affairs at all"—and so we have the overall impression of two or more friends enjoying each others' company, who must share some outlook or project in common but who also remain strangely "uninvolved" and distant from each other at the most significant level of personal interaction.[15]

Much recent work in psychology suggests that this picture would adequately characterize most friendships between men. According to Lillian Rubin and Letty Pogrebin, what counts as male friendship in modern society *is* characterized primarily by doing things together.[16] And although such friends will enjoy each others' company, they tend to remain quite guarded about their emotional life and would usually avoid any significant personal disclosure that might establish an uncomfortable intimacy between them. C. S. Lewis suggests, quite intelligently, that fear of homosexuality may lie behind the typical male discomfort with any show of physical affection with friends of the same sex. But he seems to accept, inconsistently, that the explicit avoidance of any emotional or spiritual intimacy between two friends—as opposed to a general feeling of "ease"—is a defining feature of friendship itself.

By all contemporary accounts, however, the male paradigm of friendship is no longer a satisfactory one, even and especially for men themselves. Lillian Rubin and other writers show over and over how the lack of personal intimacy in male friendships is quite marked in comparison with friendships between women. As Rubin notes, "The results of my own research are unequivocal: At every life stage between thirty-five and fifty-five, women have more friendships, as distinct from collegial relationships or work-mates, than men, and the differences in the content and quality of their friendships are marked and unmistakable."[17] Later, she cites the astonishing statistic that "in sharp contrast to the women, over two-thirds of the single men could not name a best friend," and she offers considerable evidence to suggest that on the whole, women are much more satisfied with the quality of their friend-ships than men are.[18]

I have argued that at its most basic level, friendship involves mutual recognition. Indeed, it is perhaps the most valued form of recognition since it is freely given (without biological constraint) and entails the acceptance and approval of those whom *we* have chosen to value. But it also seems very clear that this process of recognition is most satisfying when it involves the most complete mutual awareness and emotional availability that is compatible with a sense of oneself as a separate agent within the world. In C. S. Lewis, as in Aristotle and other traditional accounts, friend-ship is depicted as a static relationship insofar as it emphasizes sol-idarity and existence "side by side" and minimizes the emotional and spiritual intimacy between two people that would allow them to know each other in a more dynamic and ongoing way. Hence, it is ironic that according to most of the traditional accounts it is *women* who are incapable of friendship. Montaigne, for example, explains that "[t]he ordinary capacity of women is inadequate for that communion and fellowship which is the nurse of this sacred bond; nor does their soul seem firm enough to endure the strain of so tight and durable a knot," and he affirms "[t]he common agree-ment of the ancient schools" that women are therefore excluded from this highest possibility of life.[19]

In response to this, it can be urged that those qualities more often associated with women's friendships—emotional support, self-disclosure, and nurturing—are precisely those that deepen and intensify the process of recognition that friendship is built on. These elements are not at all incompatible with Aristotle's basic account of what friendship is, but I think they are suppressed in his work, and in other discussions of friendship, because they appear to violate the underlying ideals of self-sufficiency and sovereign self-containment. Today, we are more likely to accept that selfhood is not an original state of being, and that we come to recognize and know ourselves primarily through our dealings with other people. This means that a real involvement with someone else, in which there would be a mutual openness, trust, and emotional availability, does not have to lead to self-abandonment or self-loss. In fact, the intimate knowledge and involvement with another that is offered by friendship is more likely to provoke a deeper level of self-awareness and self-esteem; hence, it is productive of autonomy itself.

Friendship and Commitment

The ancient philosophers apparently took it for granted that friendship is an essentially moral activity. In classical antiquity, friendship was revered as one of the highest values, and it looms large in most accounts of what it means to live a good life. In Aristotle, for example, the highest form of friendship, or complete friendship, between the best kind of men is to be understood as a mutual involvement and incitement to virtue. According to Aristotle, such a friendship is bound to endure since virtue is itself the most enduring thing. From this it follows that true friendship offers us an apprenticeship in virtue and an everyday training in the moral life. We might say that friendship involves loving or liking a particular person. But for the ancients friendship was just as important for allowing individuals to cultivate the habits of generosity, reliability, and justice itself. From this perspective it would make no sense to suggest that the requirements of friendship could ever come into conflict with the requirements of justice, for as Aristotle writes, "If people are friends they have no need of justice" [1155a]. Cicero mentions the case of Gracchus and Blossius, where Blossius supposedly admitted that he would have set fire to the Capitol itself if his friend had asked him to. But Cicero is quick to dismiss this as an unreasonable, if not an impossible, response: "Wrongdoing, then, is not excused if it is committed for the sake of a friend; after all, the thing that brings friends together is their conviction of each other's virtue; it is hard to keep up a friendship, if one has deserted virtue's camp."[20] In other words, friendship is an inherently moral phenomenon.

Several of the classical authors also argue that friendship is a good insofar as it provides us with numerous opportunities to perform good and noble deeds for others. Thus, Aristotle claims that in friendship we are actively concerned about the well-being of another person for his own sake. Yet at the same time he suggests that the good man uses friendship as a way of winning glory for himself:

> This is presumably true of one who dies for others. . . . He does indeed choose something great and fine for himself. He is ready to sacrifice money as long as his friends profit, for the friends gain money, while he gains what is fine, and so he awards himself the greater good. He treats honours and offices the same way; for he will sacrifice them all for his friends, since this is fine and praiseworthy for him. . . . In everything praiseworthy, then, the excellent person awards himself what is fine. [1169a]

In a similar context, Seneca asks, "For what purpose, then, do I make a man my friend?" He replies: "In order to have someone for whom I may die, whom I may follow into exile, against whose death I may stake my own life, and pay the pledge, too."[21] I suspect that this may be a very roundabout way of reconciling friendship with the traditional ideal of self-sufficiency, for it suggests that friendship is just the occasion for a higher form of egoism and showing off. This implies a real indifference to the specificity of the other person, since it could be anyone who evokes the response of virtue. But while this perspective on friendship is inadequate and clearly does not capture the mutual involvement and vulnerability that friendship entails, it is still significant as an attempt to demonstrate the connection between friendship and the requirements of virtue.

Our own attitudes toward friendship have certainly changed since the time of Aristotle and Cicero. In fact, from a contemporary perspective, friendship is not obviously about virtue at all. We choose our friends on the basis of shared interests and compatibility. We may also share some excellence in virtue, but this is not necessarily the case. We probably believe that two bad people, such as the murderers Leopold and Loeb, may still be friends with each other. Of course, I may be aware that my friend has some real moral failings and therefore adjust my expectations accordingly, but I still consider him my friend—not because I deliberately ignore certain aspects of his character, but because friendship is not necessarily about morality and virtue.

It is probably significant, then, that there usually is not an explicit ceremony that celebrates the formation of a friendship. At another time, two friends might have sworn loyalty to each other and mixed their blood to become blood brothers or sisters. In our society, however, friendship is a loose relationship that lacks fixed rules of procedure or a specific set of obligations and requirements. Marriage is often a voluntary relationship too, but the institutional forms of marriage, and our accepted ideas about it, shape our expectations of marital partners to a much greater extent. Whereas the explicit commitment of marriage is in some sense indefinitely binding, our friendships seem to prosper or wither according to the amount of time and effort we are prepared to give them, and this is a choice that we make from one day to the next. Thus we may feel loyalty to our friends and be willing to help them, but since friendship is freely chosen and not explicitly contractual in nature, it might appear that any duties that we have to our friends must derive from a previous decision to choose the extent of our involvement with them. Do I really owe it to Smith to lend him five hundred dollars when he has fallen on hard times? Does my friendship with Jones require me to visit her in prison or not? At some point, we have to choose how much our friendships mean to us and how far we are willing to go to offer help. But the apparent informality and looseness in the forms of modern friendship call its moral status into question, for we also know that a moral obligation is more than just a matter of personal choice.

Having admitted this much, however, I believe this modern account of friendship is finally misleading and deceptive. And it is important to clarify some of the ways in which friendship must still be regarded as an inherently moral activity. In fact, no account of friendship can be purely descriptive. Since friendship is a value, the description of what friendship is, or whether someone really is a good friend to someone else, must always involve at least an implicit relationship to a prescriptive ideal.

At the outset we could insist that the relationship between friendship and duty is analytic, for to be someone's friend implies by definition that we have a set of specific obligations to that person, including an emotional availability or a willingness to drop everything and help, that we would not owe to everyone. It seems obvious that by virtue of our particular relationship to them, we do have specific duties to our parents, to our children, and to those in our care. In the same way, it may be argued, we have a set of specific obligations to our friends that derives from the structure of friendship itself. Indeed, this is why Aristotle says that what is unjust becomes more unjust when it is practiced on close friends: "It is more shocking," he claims, "to rob a companion of money than to rob a fellow-citizen" [1160a]. Whether or not this is true, however, it still begs the question because it does not explain what it is about our relationship that makes us friends, or how we acquired such obligations to them even though we never promised anything.

At the same time, however, it can hardly be denied that friendship does seem to involve a commitment to another person. This need never be explicitly given or recognized at a particular time. But, insofar as we do begin to identify the joys and sorrows of another person with our own concerns and apparently endorse the enlargement of our being by choosing continued contact with him or her, then we are also creating expectations about our availability to the other person and making a commitment in the relevant sense. Certainly, there is no legal commitment, as might exist between a husband and wife, but there is still an implicit obligation that is an organic part of the relationship itself and that would still be there even if it were not recognized by one or the other of the friends. To put this differently, when I promise that I will repay the money that you lent me, I create an expectation that is equivalent to a commitment, given the institution of promise making and all that it entails. Likewise, when I spend time with someone, accept his or her help, and make myself available to that person by sharing the more intimate aspects of myself, I am also creating an expectation that is equivalent to a commitment, given the institution of friendship and all that it commonly entails. In fact, it is both a commitment to my friend and a commitment to myself: to view her as a friend and to be open and available to her, as well as to affirm the friendship as a more or less important expression of who I take myself to be, for individual identity is largely revealed through our being with others.

Let us look more closely at the first of these aspects. The psychological genesis of a friendship may be unclear, but making a free commitment to another person, and deciding to think of him or her as a friend, involves at the very least an endorsement of the kind of person that he or she is. Of course, I may make a lot of allowances for my friend, and in my own mind I may have a more limited sense of the overall significance of the relationship, but I must also recognize something valuable about the other person that makes me want to be with that person. Once our friendship progresses, I am not able to choose the level of my moral involvement with the other person, since this follows from the dialectic of the friendship itself and is something over which I have no final control.

Perhaps, in the best sense, to be friends with someone involves a level of profound trust that allows me to reveal some of the deepest and possibly most troubling aspects of myself, while requiring me to put aside at least some of my own personal beliefs and priorities in order to reach a place of mutual involvement. Friendship does not involve the willingness to do anything for the friend in order to win approval, but friendship does require a more or less profound knowledge of who my friend is, and an awareness of what it is that she seeks and values. This requires a willingness to put my own perspective and immediate needs on hold so as to overcome any inner obstacles or ingrained ways of thinking that would prevent me from really accepting my friend and getting close to her in an ongoing way. If I always insist on my own point of view, or refuse to listen, then I have not made a serious commitment to the other person in the strong sense that friendship requires. I may be friendly and helpful to the person, but at a deeper level friendship involves a mutual openness and availability in spiritual, physical, and emotional terms. This is what constitutes the shared space of friendship and allows for mutual recognition by those who are both valued and known.

Thus, to take a literary example, when David Copperfield is sent away to Salem House school after biting his stepfather, it is his friendship with James Steerforth that largely allows him to recover his self-esteem. Steerforth promises to act as David's protector, but the friendship is really founded on the mutual space and openness to each other that is created when Steerforth asks David each evening to recount to him all of the stories that he knows. Later, David comes to recognize Steerforth's imperiousness and other moral failings, and he is devastated when Steerforth runs off with Emily to ruin so many lives. But in spite of everything, he always cherishes the memory of their friendship, which expressed both the acceptance of another and the acceptance of himself.

It is important to remember, then, that friendship is not the same as romantic love, which often points in the direction of self-abandonment. It is inevitable that our friends will share some basic values and priorities with us, for this is the respect in which the friend is "another self," as Aristotle says. If we could not sense a shared understanding about anything, then we would not have a mutual space to explore. But within these limits, we must also recognize that our friends can have a different outlook on the world, a different set of priorities and perspectives, and even, to some extent, a different set of values. To be with a friend in a meaningful way must therefore involve a readiness on my part to call into question some of my own outlooks, priorities, perspectives, and values, which would itself be an expression of my commitment to our friendship. Here again, this does not require self-abandonment, let alone the total acceptance of another person's point of view in place of one's own. As Marilyn Friedman has argued, the commitment to another person that friendship signifies involves adopting a more tentative relationship to one's own ideas and commitments. If a friend has a different perspective, I am bound, both morally and psychologically, to take that seriously, and whatever my friend takes seriously becomes important to me. In *What Are Friends For?* Friedman is able to show that there is an essential connection between friendship and moral growth, since it often happens that our friends do things or perceive things in such a way that forces us to challenge our own received ideas.[22]

Most commentators on friendship have argued, like Aristotle and Cicero, that friendship and justice must inevitably lead in the same direction; alternatively, like E. M. Forster, who is frequently quoted, they may emphasize the possibility of conflict between public virtue and our own private good. As Forster writes, "If I had to choose between betraying my country and betraying my friend, I hope I should have the guts to betray my country."[23] But what is not often grasped is the sense in which most of our active moral life takes place at the intersection between our commitment to people and our commitment to particular values and principles. Usually, a friend will help us to clarify and deepen our own ideas about the world, and sometimes he or she will force us to rethink some things that we may have taken for granted.

But there may also come a point when our commitment to a friend is finally incompatible with our commitment to a particular principle. Thus, according to Shakespeare's version, Brutus loved Caesar, but in the end, his deep commitment to the Republic led him to join the conspiracy against Caesar, who wanted to be king. As opposed to Cassius, Brutus did not make this choice easily, but remained agonized by the conflicting claims of friendship and a guiding moral belief. Similarly, when Dickens describes David Copperfield's feelings after he discovers that Steerforth has gone off with Emily, he expresses quite profoundly the sense in which David's love and concern for Steerforth are irreducible to a coincidence of principles and shared ideas about the world. For even if their friendship must now be over, that love and concern will continue:

> What is natural in me is natural in many other men, I infer, and so I am not afraid to write that I never had loved Steerforth better than when the ties that bound me to him were broken. In the keen distress of the discovery of his unworthiness, I thought more of all that was brilliant in him, I softened more towards all that was good in him, I did more justice to the qualities that might have made him a man of noble nature and a great name, than ever I had done in the height of my devotion to him. Deeply as I felt my own unconscious part in his pollution of an honest home, 1 believed that if I had been brought face to face with him, I could not have uttered one reproach. I should have loved him so well still—though he fascinated me no longer—I should have held in so much tenderness the memory of my affection for him, that I think I should have been as weak as a spirit-wounded child, in all but the entertainment of a thought that we could ever be reunited. That thought I never had. I felt, as he had felt, that all was at an end between us.[24]

Dickens offers a compelling account of the emotional complexity involved in David's response to Steerforth's unworthiness. In this case, the repudiation of their friendship does seem to be morally appropriate. In other circumstances, though, it may also be possible to trust another person and accept his or her point of view so completely that we will jettison a moral principle that we formerly accepted. I may be morally opposed to homosexuality, for example, but if my good friend says that he is gay and argues against my opposition to homosexuality with thought and passion, I may not drop him as a friend or condemn him even though he does not accept my own moral standards. Indeed, because this is someone that I deeply respect and care about, I may be prepared to reconsider what I think about homosexuality insofar as I am prepared to view things from his perspective. In fact, I am *bound* to do so because he is my friend and I trust the kind of person that he is. Through my friendships, then, I will continue to experience moral transformation and growth.

It may be objected that this openness to other views is a form of moral abandonment and a retreat from personal responsibility, inasmuch as being truly authentic involves having the courage of our own convictions and not being swayed or unduly influenced by the actions of others, including, presumably, our friends. But such a response really implies a complete devotion to the tyranny of principles and the unreflective endorsement of one particular way of thinking about morality. It further assumes that all other principles outrank the moral value of being a good friend. Sometimes we must find the courage to challenge our convictions and whatever prejudices we may have grown up with. The logic of friendship requires us to place our commitments to people and our commitments to principles on a somewhat equal footing. It is not the case that one of them must always have priority over the other. We do not abandon all personal responsibility for our actions and beliefs once we choose to view things from the perspective of a friend.

This leads us, then, to the second aspect of our commitment to our friends. In friendship, we commit ourselves to another person by giving that person the promise of physical and emotional support. But in friendship, we also make a commitment to ourselves, insofar as we view our own activity within the friendship as an important and undeniable manifestation of who we are. Our commitment to our friends is one of the first things that opens us up to the moral life and provides us with a strong sense of ourselves as active moral beings. We do not choose the families that we are born into or all of the obligations that may be assigned to any given social role, such as that of child or sister. But we do choose who our friends are, and the level of our involvement with them. In this respect, we are making a commitment to ourselves, insofar as we are choosing to understand ourselves in a particular way by actively cultivating a particular set of friends.

It might be held that making a commitment to oneself is only a very weak and derivative form of a genuine moral commitment. As a New Year's resolution, for example, I may promise myself that I will read Hegel every day for the rest of the year, but if I fail to keep my resolution I am not really hurting anyone except, possibly, myself. As it is, since I was the one who decided not to go ahead with it, I have only done what I wanted to do. In the case of making and keeping friends, however, I think that something much deeper than this is at stake. Whereas I may be upset with myself for not keeping my resolution, in failing to be a good friend I am also threatening the most basic and undeniable representation of who I am insofar as this emerges in my relationship with others. It seems obvious, in fact, that our self-esteem and self-knowledge come to us through the mediation of other people. We could not know ourselves nearly as well if we had no intimate companions with whom we could share our inner lives. Furthermore, it would be much harder to esteem and value ourselves if no one valued our existence or cared about us as particular beings. As we have seen, Aristotle insists that a friend is "another self," someone who shares many of the same values and priorities and goals as we do. Insofar as the other person affirms me as a friend, the other person is also reflecting back to me an approval and an endorsement of who I am.

In this sense, then, friendship is all about mutual recognition. The self that we understand ourselves to be is not developed in isolation but in our ongoing relationships with other people, especially with our friends who know us best. Thus the duties of friendship, such as availability, caring, and nurturing, are duties that we owe to someone else insofar as we are committed to that person. At the same time, albeit indirectly, these are also duties that we owe it to ourselves to fulfill. The requirements of friendship provide some of the most basic conditions that support our own continuing sense of personal identity and self-worth. We are all concerned with the kind of people that we are, and our strongest sense of who we are is developed in our ongoing relations with other people, especially with our friends. In brief, our commitment to friendship is an objective expression of our commitment to the moral life. Indeed, at a more basic level than the reflective choice of moral principles and explicit values, my friends give me recognition and make me immediately aware of myself as an active moral being.

By choosing to cultivate certain friendships and pursuing them in different ways, I have effectively chosen to think of myself, and to let others think of me, in a certain way. The self that is clarified through our friendships is in some ways an ideal self, insofar as it becomes something that we seek to live up to if we are in any way concerned about our own moral standing. When the demands of friendship are overwhelming, we will persevere because we sense that we would be letting ourselves down if we simply gave up. To betray a friend to the enemy—for example, to abandon him out of fear when you could have hidden him in your house—is also to destroy the positive representation of yourself that has emerged through the course of your friendship with him. It might be suggested cynically that we really do not care about what other people think and that every friendship is based on self-interest in a narrow sense. But if I have entered into a friendship with another person, then I have shown that what that person thinks is important to me, and his or her perception of me is an irresistible and constitutive aspect of who I am. Friendship involves a commitment both to myself and to others, and as a moral being I am bound to recognize and honor that commitment. In a case like that of Brutus, we may decide that one of these commitments must cancel out the other. But with this example, we return to Cicero's point that friendship can never be opposed to virtue, even if the relationship between friendship and virtue must still remain unclear.

It may be formally correct to say that friendship, unlike marriage, does not involve any obvious contractual obligations. I cannot be punished if I choose to give up on my friends, although I may be punished if I desert my family. Despite this, however, I have shown two ways in which friendship is and must remain an essentially moral phenomenon. First, friendship involves a commitment to another person that implies openness and availability. To become unavailable to the other person by refusing help or emotional support may be viewed as a moral failing within that context. In this respect, and at any other level than mere acquaintanceship, friendship is one of the most important contexts for moral development and growth. Aristotle knew this, but he also presupposed a univocal conception of the higher good. This no longer exists, if it ever did, and indeed communities of friends will often arise as forms of affirmation and avowal in opposition to traditional establishment norms. But the moral horizon still emerges most clearly and forcefully in our commitments to our friends, in our commitments to our own values and beliefs, and in the relationship between these.

Second, friendship involves an implicit commitment to ourselves. One thing that emerges in our friendships with other people is the sense that "this is the person that I want to be." To betray a friend, or even just to let her down, is therefore to repudiate a positive image of who we are, an image that is available both to ourselves and to others. And if we say we do not care, then so much the worse for us, since this would be a measure of our own self-loss and a sign of unconcern about ourselves that would be hard to comprehend. In fact, if we have any concern at all about our own moral worth, then we are bound to try to be good friends since friendship significantly determines our own self-understanding and sense of self-esteem.

As we have seen, in his own work on friendship, Aristotle tries to show at one point how friendship toward others is ultimately derived from the features of friendship toward oneself. Some readers may see in this an attempt to derive altruism from egoism, but given that Aristotle also says in this section that the friend is "another himself," we should be suspicious of any interpretation that fixes the self and then emphasizes its complete distinction from all others, including our friends. In friendship the openness and availability to others unfixes all of the boundaries of the self.

Similarly, in his moral philosophy, Kant distinguishes between the two general categories of duties to ourselves and duties to others. Once again, this is a static way of thinking about these things, but it must be allowed that friendship is a domain of moral experience that evokes duties toward others as well as duties toward ourselves. At the same time, though, it has to be said that friendship also implies an enlargement of our own personal identity and circle of concern, as well as a readiness to call that identity into question, or at least not to insist on it, for the sake of our friend. Thus the shared horizon of friendship unsettles the fixed opposition between self and other. This should lead us to consider how our commitments and duties to others might actually follow from an implicit commitment toward ourselves, while any commitment to ourselves can only be understood in the context of our meaningful being with others. At some level, this is what the ancient commentators on friendship understood. Despite their extreme attachment to traditional ideals of self-sufficiency and autarchy, they were also aware of the problematic status of friendship, which promises self-fulfillment while it also requires the ethical subordination of the self to something that exceeds it.

Friendship and Contemporary Life

Finally, then, what are we to make of the significance or role of friendship in contemporary life? For the ancients, friendship was absolutely important and was viewed, at least by Aristotle, as the basic social cement that contributed to the overall solidarity of society. Today, it is more likely that we will make a sharp distinction between the public and the private domains of human life, and we will view friendship as a private affair that is not necessarily connected to the greater good of the state. Perhaps, then, as some writers have suggested, the decline of friendship in contemporary society is related to the decline of political life, for if commitment to the public good is not considered primary or absolute, then any friendships that do emerge must be based on partial and transitory interests and cannot assume a common ground that all must inevitably share. Thus it will be said that in our culture we must look for fulfillment within the family and through romantic love. Friendship is still relevant, but as C. S. Lewis suggests, "it is something quite marginal; not a main course in life's banquet, [but] a diversion; something that fills up the chinks of one's time."[25]

Briefly, and in conclusion, I propose the following three points, which presuppose that there will always be a difference between the lived reality of friendship and friendship as a possible ideal of social life that could still be inspiring. First, like every other kind of love, friendship is absolutely important to us and existentially significant insofar as it releases us from the isolation of individual existence and opens us to others. Today, romantic love is a much more dominant and popular value than friendship. But romantic love also tends toward self-abandonment, and so it does not often lead to self-knowledge or self-understanding except accidentally, when it has run its course and the lovers can stand back to try to understand what happened. In friendship, on the other hand, mutual recognition must lead to self-understanding and an awareness of the other person as an end in himself. In friendship the self may be challenged but never abandoned; in this way, friendship allows the individual to grow in moral understanding and to achieve a depth of awareness that seems to run counter to the prevailing tendencies of contemporary life.

Second, even though we live in a pluralistic society, it is not the case that in comparison with the Greeks our friendships are bound to be limited and inadequate. There is still a relationship between genuine friendship and community, but it is not the same relationship that apparently prevailed in the time of Aristotle. For many people today, there is no real sense of "the community" in general. Perhaps our society is just too large, and perhaps we are suspicious that any single account of the common good may also serve as a basis for repression and control. In any case, community in the strong sense of something to which we experience a sense of belonging is seldom given to us; more than ever, perhaps, it is something that we have to create for ourselves. As an example of this, Lillian Rubin considers contemporary networks of friendships between gays and lesbians. Such friendships are a way of creating an alternative community of concern for those who are frequently outcast by the traditional community itself.[26] Other examples might be given, but the point is that here, as in Aristotle, the community created by friendship allows individuals to affirm themselves and recover their own self-worth. In this respect, friendship remains an essential aspect of the political and allows us to avoid the domination of consumerism and other forms of selfish individualism.

Third, in opposition to Aristotle, we must emphasize the differences between individuals—the fact that we are specific and unique—as a driving force in the dynamic of friendship. As we have seen, recognition in the deepest sense presupposes alterity. This means that in genuine friendship one must always have a strong sense of the friend as another person—not as a barrier to be negotiated but never known, but as a singular and unique individual that we can become more or less involved with. We can only grow in self-awareness and self-understanding as we open ourselves and become more available to this other person. What we miss with the ancients is a strong sense of the specific being of the other person, the possibility of mutual growth through tension and difference, and the particularity of the relationship that Montaigne will later evoke in his profound line "Because it was he, because it was I."[27] In this respect, the friend is more than just a second self. He or she is also experienced as a mystery and as someone who *is* "wholly other." Any account of the good of friendship must include this sense of wonder concerning the other person, for it is this which first arrests us, and in the end it is only this which breaks the circuits of our own self-involvement.

2

The Value of Romantic Love

Romantic lovers inhabit a world of their own. Typically, this is portrayed as a very private world of intense passion and personal significance that is totally removed from the everyday realm to which we are usually confined. The ideal exemplars of romantic love—such as Romeo and Juliet, Tristan and Isolde, or Cathy and Heathcliff—are completely focused on each other, and in their abiding desire for one another they experience a shared identity as lovers that seems to outweigh their own separation as individual selves. Romantic lovers experience bliss and exaltation when they abandon the petty concerns of their selfish lives to devote themselves entirely to love. And like Werther, who proclaims his passion for Lotte in absolute terms—"I have no prayers left except prayers to her, my imagination calls up no other image than hers, and I see everything in the world only in relation to her"[1]—they must endure a total reorientation of perspective and the loss of self-rule as they are literally overwhelmed by love. Lovers such as Werther must suffer anguish and despair when their love is not returned; even in the face of death, however, they yearn for "fusion," or a blissful melting of souls that would somehow redeem the senseless character of individual life and make their existence meaningful.

From one perspective, then, the ideal of romantic love is absolutely valuable and important since it is an expression of the most complete intensification and exaltation of life possible. Romantic lovers seem to be ennobled by their passion. Their love is an affirmation of human existence, and it represents an absolute refusal to allow their destiny to be controlled by the impersonal forces of society or convention, or even reason itself.

45

Especially when one perceives the society in which one lives to be totally corrupt and soul-destroying, romantic love may be viewed as a defiant and transfiguring force that reasserts the value of human life in both its spiritual and its physical aspects. This is obviously the case with the love of Romeo and Juliet, set against the moribund world of competing Veronese dynasties. Perhaps even more so in the modern world, in opposition to all of the calculations of instrumental reason and the increasing commodification of every aspect of human life, romantic love appears absolutely valuable because it does not calculate and it never treats passion as an investment that requires a return. On the contrary, romantic love is an act of pure generosity because it involves the complete giving of oneself and the cherishing and idealizing of another person that bestows an absolute value upon him or her. Romantic love promises us an escape from the pain of isolation and the possibility of sharing our deepest and most intimate selves. However excessive the pronouncements of romantic lovers may be, in this respect their love is a celebration of life and promotes the unity that underlies beings who are only apparently separate.[2]

This leads us, though, to a second perspective on romantic love. The *image* of romantic love is certainly alluring—and in our culture such love is typically viewed as an essential ingredient of personal happiness—but it may be argued that romantic love is also a myth that allows us to avoid the problems of the real world by escaping into a private realm of fantasy. Stendhal believed that "passion love," as he called it, was the most important thing in life because it gives us the most exhilarating experience and the sense of being truly alive. But even he seems to admit that this kind of love is saturated with illusions and exists more as an object of reverie in the mind of the lover, who projects ideal qualities onto his or her beloved.[3] In his *Liber Amoris*, William Hazlitt gives a rather painful account of his own romantic obsession for the unexceptional young woman he fell madly in love with. He tells her:

> Your ordinary walk is as if you were performing some religious ceremony; you come up to my table of a morning, when you merely bring in the tea-things, as if you were advancing to the altar. You move in minuet-time: you measure every step, as if you were afraid of offending in the smallest things. I never hear your approach on the stairs, but by a sort of hushed silence. When you enter the room, the Graces wait on you, and Love waves round your person in gentle undulations, breathing balm into the soul! By Heaven, you are an

angel! You look like one at this instant! Do I not adore you—and have I merited this return?⁴

In *The Sorrows of Young Werther*, the hero describes his own passion for Lotte in equally worshipful terms: "She is sacred to me," he exclaims. "Any desire is silenced in her presence. I never know what I feel when I am with her; it is as if my soul were spinning through every nerve. She plays a melody on her clavichord with the touch of an angel, so simple, so ethereal! It is her favorite tune, and I am cured of all pain, confusion, and melancholy the moment she strikes the first note."⁵ By multiplying examples like these, we can easily draw out the self-indulgent aspect of romantic love. Cynically, we might add that when this love is requited it actually becomes harder to bear, for the reality of a lived involvement with another person is unnerving insofar as it threatens the romantic ideal that we have already projected for ourselves.

Thus, romantic lovers forget about the real world, and in their total devotion to their own passion they are even capable of the worst actions, since they hold the rule of love to be more important and more pressing than anything else. When Anna Karenina kills herself at the end of Tolstoy's novel we do feel some compassion for her, and given the way that she has been abandoned by her lover, we may even accept that in her distress this was the only outcome that was possible for her. But at the same time, her romantic involvement with Vronsky is the immediate cause of her own despair and the future misery of her son and other survivors. Romantic lovers inhabit a world of their own. Insofar as they are compelled by their love and cultivate their own passionate attachment to each other, they are not ruled by reason, and they remain unconcerned about the ordinary duties and responsibilities that bind us to the rest of human society.

But in what sense is romantic love a relevant ideal? Or should we say that it is primarily a literary value that allows us to escape from the problems of real life? Something like romantic love has probably existed in most societies. The ancient Egyptians, Hebrews, and Persians all had their own love poetry, and in Plato especially, the yearning of the lover is described and even celebrated as an opening onto the divine. But it is only recently, in the modern age, that romantic love has become a massive phenomenon and a dominant cultural theme. The stories of Lancelot and Guinevere or Romeo and Juliet suggest that romantic love was at one time something exceptional that challenged the established order and the priority of duty and blood. But romantic love has now become a popular expectation, and today we tend to assume that a life lived without romantic experience must be wretched and unfulfilled. So even if we regard Romeo and Juliet and all of the others as excessive romantic projections, we must also accept that they are the expressions of an ideal that has helped to condition much of our thinking and even our experience of passionate love today. The continued popularity and appeal of such works is precisely because they respond to and articulate a certain way of thinking about passionate love that is still prevalent.

Thus romantic love remains an important value in our culture. But we must now ask, what is the value of this value? Does it ultimately lead to human fulfillment and the empowerment of individual lives, or does it promote alienation and emotional distress? Should we preserve romantic love as an ideal that we can always aspire toward, even if its pure form can never be reached? Or should we abandon it as a pernicious ideal that creates unreasonable expectations of happiness that can never be fulfilled?

To begin to answer these questions, we must first discuss some of the most typical features of what is commonly referred to as "romantic love." This is not to specify an exclusive set of necessary and sufficient conditions, however, since this would imply that romantic love is a univocal phenomenon. The truth is that romantic love is completely *overdetermined* and has a variety of origins in the historical, psychological, and economic realities of everyday life. And so, while it is the case that something *like* romantic love may be found in other cultures, it is significant that romantic love itself—as opposed to Platonic love or courtly love and so forth— has only become a popular idea since the beginning of the modern age. We must therefore examine the overall place of romantic love within the total economy of our culture and ask why it has become such a grand ideal. None of this is to assert or to deny that in any given case, romantic love may be beneficial. But here we are concerned with the overall tendency of romantic love within society itself.

Two themes will be crucial to the discussion that follows. The first is the respect in which passionate love in general involves an idealizing of the beloved that radically transforms and transfigures the life of the lover. Here, we will note that romantic love in particular is subtended by attitudes and postures that are basically religious in nature, for the adoration of the beloved is very closely related to the religious adoration of God. The second point concerns the shared identity that romantic lovers insist on, which is poetically expressed by the images of merging, melting, and fusion. In fact, this shared identity, or romance, is projected as the *truth* of the individual lovers, who are then held to be incomplete without each other. At a certain point, however, the idealization of the beloved will come into conflict with this valorization of the romantic relationship itself, which leads to the end of self-transformation and to the lover's attempt to appropriate and control the beloved. This conclusion concerns the specific failure of romantic love.

Nevertheless, I do not want to claim that erotic love itself is based on a contradiction, and in the second part of this chapter I sketch another model of passionate involvement, or postromantic love. It is perhaps necessary to be more speculative here because to the extent that we are still constrained by romantic structures we simply lack the vocabulary that would clearly describe the possibilities that lie beyond romantic loving. But at this point in history, the discussion of postromantic love remains extremely important, and it may evoke a more authentic paradigm for understanding and appropriating our own passionate lives. The chapter concludes by offering a verdict on the present and future value of romantic and postromantic love.

The Structure of Romantic Love

At the outset, it may be said that there is no essential connection between erotic desire and love. For desire may exist as a purely physical impulse without attendant feelings of affection, and there are certain forms of love, such as friendship or parental love, that are not obviously informed by physical desire. This might suggest that love and desire must be two separate streams, and in both philosophical and religious thinking on the matter, they have often been viewed as hostile to each other.[6] This is apparently the case for Plato, when he views physical desire as something that must be superseded if love is to achieve its highest fulfillment, and also for Christianity, when it emphasizes the absolute conflict between the spiritual love of God and the carnal desire for another as the conflict between our higher and lower natures. The latter position is stated most famously by St. Paul: "In my inmost self I delight in the law of God, but I perceive that there is in my bodily members a different law, fighting against the law that my reason approves and making me a prisoner under the law that is in my members, the law of sin."[7] More recently, the discourse of "sexual liberation" celebrates an unencumbered sexuality that seems to reinforce the separation between sexual desire and love. For this reason, it remains difficult to reflect clearly on erotic or passionate love, which is that region of human experience where love and physical desire *do* converge and intensify each other. Even so, over the course of history various ideals of passionate love have been developed and embraced, including the Greek account of eros, the courtly love tradition of the Middle Ages, and the modern ideal of romantic love.

"Erotic" or "passionate" love is focused on physical embodiment. The erotic lover is intensely aware and even preoccupied with the physical being of his or her beloved. But this is not the same kind of awareness with which we appreciate the comforting physical presence of a friend, or the reassuring embrace of a parent or a child. In fact, the erotic lover experiences a heightened perception of every nuance and detail that constitutes the beloved's embodied form. In the lover's desire and rapture, the beloved is cherished and even transfigured as the focus of meaning and value. In *Death in Venice,* for example, Thomas Mann captures something of this when he describes von Aschenbach's obsession for the youth, Tadzio: "Soon the observer knew every line and pose of this form that limned itself so freely against sea and sky; its every loveliness, though conned by heart, yet thrilled him each day afresh; his admiration knew no bounds, the delight of his eye was unending." Von Aschenbach views Tadzio as the paragon of beauty, and his detailed description of the boy celebrates the radiance of his physical form:

> The ringlets of honey-coloured hair clung to his temples and neck, the fine down along the upper vertebrae was yellow in the sunlight; the thin envelope of flesh covering the torso betrayed the delicate outlines of the ribs and the symmetry of the breast structure. His armpits were still as smooth as a statue's, smooth the glistening hollows behind the knees, where the blue network of veins suggested that the body was formed of some stuff more transparent than mere flesh. What discipline, what precision of thought were expressed by the tense youthful perfection of this form![8]

Now perhaps it is the beauty of the boy that first incites von Aschenbach's erotic longing. But at the same time, it must be said that von Aschenbach's desire serves to idealize and transfigure Tadzio so that he becomes, for von Aschenbach, the absolute perfection of physical form. And this is significant: Erotic love is always experienced as a destiny, and never as a rational decision or as the free choice of the will. Von Aschenbach initially takes the stance of the detached connoisseur of beauty. But in the end, it becomes clear that he is also overwhelmed. Erotic love disturbs and even humiliates our sense of self-possession. We must either endure this extreme abjection of being or else moralize and justify our passions as a way of redeeming ourselves from the contingency into which we have fallen. Thus, for the erotic lover, and especially the romantic lover, the beloved becomes the most perfect being in the world, or the "one and only," who is worthy of the most extreme sacrifice and devotion. And this is only to echo and support Plato's insistence on the mutual implication of goodness, truth, and beauty on the level of the individual.

In his book *On Love*, Stendhal discusses this theme with his famous theory of "crystallization," in which he compares the idealizing tendency of romantic passion to the shining crystals that will eventually encrust an ordinary branch when it is thrown into a salt mine. The analogy occurs to him after he watches a young officer who is clearly in the first stages of falling in love:

> What struck me was the undertone of madness which grew moment by moment in the discourse of the officer; each moment he saw in this woman perfections more and more invisible to my eyes. Each moment what he said bore *less resemblance* to the woman he was beginning to love. I thought to myself: "La Ghita is certainly no more than a pretext for all the raptures of this poor German." For example he began to praise Madame Gherardi's hand, which had been curiously marked by smallpox in her childhood and had remained very pocked and rather brown.
> "How shall I explain what I see?" I wondered. "Where shall I find a comparison to illustrate my thought?"[9]

By way of an answer, Stendhal explains that in "passion love" we always view the beloved not as he or she *really* is, but through pleasurable illusions that we project to flatter our passion. And this is the reason why, "on the moral plane," he comments elsewhere, "love is the strongest of the passions. In all the others, desires have to adapt themselves to cold reality, but in love realities obligingly rearrange themselves to conform with desire. There is therefore more scope for the indulgence of violent desires in love than in any other passion."[10]

Thus, specific qualities of the beloved are enhanced and transfigured through the lover's attention and rapture. The lover is *bound* to recognize the beloved as beautiful and to cherish the distinctive qualities that seem to express his or her unique and unrepeatable being. But at the same time, and just as significantly, these physical qualities are also revalued as the obvious bodily manifestations of goodness and moral character. In romantic love, the physical features of the beloved tend to acquire a meaning and a spiritual significance as we moralize our desire. We may find that the face of the one that we love seems to express an absolute kindness, or we may see in the mouth or the eyes of the beloved the perfect manifestation of generosity and goodness. In *Death in Venice*, von Aschenbach is impressed by the nobility and graciousness that Tadzio's physical bearing appears to express. The point is that in this kind of passion the focus on the other person is complete. Not only is his or her physical being cherished as beautiful, but the beloved's ideal spiritual or moral being is experienced through his or her physical form and may even become an object of physical desire itself. Such a love thereby erases the strict distinction between the carnal and the spiritual aspects of the self that has been such an enduring feature of the Western intellectual tradition.

We could say, then, that the goodness of erotic love consists in the value that it brings into the world, for in cherishing the beloved it bestows meaning and significance where none had existed before. Moreover, passionate love seems to enlarge the soul by opening us up to the absolute significance of another person. This is a tumultuous encounter that can empower and transfigure our own lives by wrenching us out of our everyday contentment and forcing us to experience our own existence with an intensity that is not usually present. The self in love, we might say, is a self-in-process—no longer at ease with itself or self-absorbed and apparently self-contained, but open toward another and ready to receive its truth from outside. In this respect, to fall in love is to experience something similar to the dislocation and rapture that one might experience with a powerful religious conversion. And even though we must experience the disorientation that accompanies the relinquishing of personal control, we can look forward with enhanced expectation to a new phase in the development of our lives.

Plato recognized the absolute importance of erotic love as an experience that draws us out of ourselves and orients us toward the divine. He argues that in the first stirring of erotic love we are really inspired by the intimation of eternity that the beloved evokes. When Socrates explains the real nature of love in the *Sym-*

posium, he systematically describes the various stages of its existence, beginning with the love of the beautiful individual and culminating with the love of the Good, which is immutable and beyond space and time. Socrates' discussion of erotic love in the *Symposium* is famously problematic, for in his account the individual beloved is apparently *not* cherished for his or her own sake, but is used as the means for achieving a higher Good where individuals are irrelevant. From this perspective, I do not love the one whom I love as a unique and unrepeatable being who has both virtues and flaws. I am inspired and directed only by the estimable qualities of the beloved—such as physical beauty—and this makes the beloved entirely substitutable with others who also have those qualities. In response we might ask, Can it really be "love" if at some level one's desire already contains a willingness to relinquish or subordinate the beloved to a "more important" goal?

Elsewhere, in the *Phaedrus,* Plato views erotic love between two individuals as a problem that must be corrected once it is more fully understood. Socrates is enamored of Phaedrus and is totally distracted by desire for him. But he *uses* this passion to achieve his marvelous vision of the eternal procession and the image of the charioteer who drives the good and bad horses of the soul. Once again, it seems that something other than love has become love's goal:

> So when they lie side by side the wanton horse of the lover's soul would have a word with the charioteer, claiming a little guerdon for all his trouble. The like steed in the soul of the beloved has no word to say, but, swelling with desire for he knows not what, embraces and kisses the lover, in grateful acknowledgement of all his kindness. And when they lie by one another, he is minded not to refuse to do his part in gratifying his lover's entreaties; yet his yokefellow in turn, being moved by reverence and heedfulness, joins with the driver in resisting. And so, if the victory be won by the higher elements of mind guiding them into the ordered rule of the philosophical life, their days on earth will be blessed with happiness and concord, for the power of evil in the soul has been subjected, and the power of goodness liberated; they have won self-mastery and inward peace.[11]

Here, the Platonic vision affirms the principle of self-commandment even while it is inspired by the loss of self-control that eros represents. In both the *Phaedrus* and the *Symposium,* the *final* goal is the serene contemplation of philosophy, and sovereign self-sufficiency.

As the inevitable prelude to this philosophical detachment and calm, the madness of erotic love is thereby redeemed and justified.

Traditional "romantic" literature apprehends erotic love with similar categories and forms of understanding. But in one significant respect, it can be argued that romantic love marks an advance over the Platonic perspective insofar as it celebrates the erotic love of *particular* individuals as something that is absolutely valuable in itself. Both Plato and the romantics try to justify erotic love by showing its link to the eternal and ideal. In Plato, erotic love is the first step away from our ordinary selfish concerns, and the first movement toward the divine order of things. In romantic love, however, love itself is divine, and the beloved is revalued as an absolute ideal. And whether or not we are ourselves responsible for this illusion, as Stendhal seems to imply, we are thereby given access to the infinite and eternity itself through the beloved. Hazlitt writes:

> When I press her hand, I enjoy perfect happiness and contentment of soul. It is not what she says or what she does—it is herself that I love. To be with her is to be at peace. I have no other wish or desire. The air about her is serene, blissful; and he who breathes it is like one of the Gods! so that I can but have her with me always, I care for nothing more. I never could tire of her sweetness; I feel that I could grow to her, body and soul, my heart, my heart is her's.[12]

Of course, Hazlitt's lines are excessive, and they reveal something of his own abjection. But in this passage, he gives direct expression to the typical romantic yearning for a complete union and merging with the beloved that would grant the calm of eternity.

In this way, the ideal romantic lover exalts the beloved as the unique focus of value. For the lover, this is the sense in which the beloved really does become the whole world, and as the lover begins to see everything through the eyes of the beloved, every aspect of life becomes important or irrelevant insofar as it is related to the latter. Thus, if we say that in Plato's account of love the beloved is apparently devalued and used as the means to a more important end, we should also admit that the romantic account of love may actually involve the opposite difficulty, in which the romantic beloved is completely *overvalued* to the point of being worshipped as an absolute ideal. Romantic love encourages the postures of devotion and submission and is driven by a longing for salvation and the desire for eternity itself. It seems to require a total self-abandonment and the exaltation of the other person, and it must regard any other considerations as irrelevant or even opposed to the requirements of love. "Let Rome in Tiber melt!" says Shakespeare's Mark Antony, for the world means nothing to him while he is under the spell of Cleopatra. Such attitudes might be appropriate in a religious context, but when they are prescriptively imposed on the meaning of erotic love, they diminish the possibilities of reflection and distance and entail a kind of moral oblivion. Even if one could just forget about the rest of the world, this perspective is spiritually and emotionally disfiguring for each of the individuals involved.

Let us consider the religious attitudes that subtend romantic love in some more detail. First, a strong part of the allure of romantic love lies in its powerful expressions of complete and unconditional devotion to the beloved. Romantic lovers promise undying love and the total sacrifice of their own lives for the sake of the other, if this is what is required; and the intensity of their passion is often expressed in terms of their obliviousness to everything else. Hence in Stendhal, "I felt with a rush of pride and delight that my love was far greater than his. I told myself that those cheeks would grow pale with fear at even the least of the sacrifices my love would joyfully make. For instance, I would gladly plunge my hand into a hat to take out one of two tickets: 'be loved by her' or 'Die at once.' "[13] With this devotion, this depth of feeling, and scorn of ordinary constraints and conventions, romantic lovers aspire toward the infinite and eternity through the mediation of the beloved. This makes perfect amatory sense, for as long as the beloved is taken as an absolute ideal the lover *must* be absolutely devoted and inspired.

Similarly, romantic love involves a deep, and sometimes desperate, yearning for the beloved that is not usually present in friendship or other kinds of love. In romantic love one experiences oneself as distracted and no longer under one's own control. The yearning of romantic love thereby signifies the gap between the absolute valorization of the beloved and the low estimation of the self that emerges by comparison. For the one who is in love, the beloved seems to promise access to a region of serenity and fulfillment that has so far been denied. The lover is filled with longing to achieve this goal. "Oh, this void, this terrifying void I feel in my breast!" Werther cries. "I often think: if you could once, only once, press her to your heart, this void would be filled."[14] Like other romantic lovers, Werther suffers from a sense of incompletion and inadequacy, and he yearns for Lotte as the unique and irreplaceable other who promises salvation and fulfillment. His whole reason for living and his sense of self-worth are now dependent on Lotte's response. But the question can be asked, In what sense *is* this the deepest manifestation of love for someone else? It suggests that such a love is really inspired by a hidden theological need, which divinizes the beloved and enjoins devotion and self-sacrifice for the sake of eternity and salvation from ourselves. In the end, however, this is actually to avoid the real encounter with another human being.

Such a love is thus deeply problematic. There is, of course, a sense in which the projection of ideal qualities onto the beloved can have a self-fulfilling effect. If I see you as absolutely fair and kind, then you may strive even harder to live up to this ideal portrait that I have of you, and so you may actually become worthy of my praise. But at some point, idealization becomes falsification. The romantic tendency, as in Hazlitt or in Werther's impossible passion, is to idolize and divinize the beloved to an impossible degree; this kind of erotic projection misses the real individual, who has both strengths and weaknesses, and cultivates a phantom instead. In fact, it may be said that romantic lovers are too often enthralled with the *idea* of love. They cultivate the *state* of being in love and they project romantic horizons, while remaining indifferent to the actual needs of the beloved. And in this respect, romantic love becomes a selfish preoccupation, in which the beloved is secondary.

At the outset, I argued that romantic love derives from the underlying desire of the subject to share a world with the beloved and to be the focus of the beloved's concern. The literature of romantic love is filled with images and ideas of merging, melting, and fusion that express the lovers' desire to overcome the limitations of their particular identity. In the *Symposium*, Aristophanes is one of the popular exponents of this theme when he argues in his comic speech that "We used to be complete wholes in our original nature, and now 'Love' is the name for our pursuit of wholeness, for our desire to be complete."[15]

Later, the same idea receives a very serious philosophical and poetical treatment in the writings of the Romantics: Keats, Shelley, Novalis, and numerous others. Shelley, for example, elevates love into a cosmic force that binds everything together by overcoming all separation and difference. In *Epipsychidion*, he very powerfully describes a physical and a spiritual intermingling that would be the final consummation of romantic love:

> Our breath shall intermix, our bosoms bound,
> And our veins beat together; and our lips
> With other eloquence than words, eclipse
> The soul that burns between them, and the wells
> Which boil under our being's inmost cells,
> The fountains of our deepest life, shall be
> Confused in Passion's golden purity,
> As mountain-springs under the morning sun.
> We shall become the same, we shall be one
> Spirit within two frames, oh! wherefore two?
> One passion in twin-hearts, which grows and grew,
> Till like two meteors of expanding flame,
> Those spheres instinct with it become the same,
> Touch, mingle, are transfigured; ever still
> Burning, yet ever inconsummable:
> In one another's substance finding food,
> Like flames too pure and light and unimbued
> To nourish their bright lives with baser prey,
> Which point to Heaven and cannot pass away:
> One hope within two wills, one will beneath
> Two overshadowing minds, one life, one death,
> One Heaven, one Hell, one immortality,
> And one annihilation.[16]

Over the years, perhaps, the sentiment behind such astonishing expressions has become more routine, and the idea of merging or fusion has become a dominant image in the vocabulary of modern romantic love. In *Women in Love*, one of D. H. Lawrence's most reflective characters describes the loss of individual identity that the authentic experience of love must entail: "Even when he said, whispering with truth, 'I love you,' 'I love you,' it was not the real truth. . . . How could he say 'I' when he was something new and unknown, not himself at all? This I, this old formula of the age was a dead letter." And he continues with a rapturous assertion of the triumph of romantic fusion:

> In the new, superfine bliss, a peace superseding knowledge, there was no I and you, there was only the third, unrealized wonder, the wonder of existing not as oneself but in a consummation of my being and of her being in a new one, a new, paradisal unit regained from the duality. How can I say "I love you" when I have ceased to be: we are both caught up and transcended into a new oneness where everything is silent, because there is nothing to answer, all is perfect and at one.[17]

Lawrence understood, like Shelley and other romantic writers before him, that the physical expression of love in erotic experience is the deepest, if not the only way, to achieve the oneness of romantic fusion. The self-dispossession that is possible in sex— the temporary suspension of every ordinary project and goal—is really a reflection, if not a culmination, of the self-abandonment that individuals must undergo in order to acquire the renewed identity of love. To abandon control of one's body in sex is to experience the physical correlate of this emotional and spiritual yielding. So here again, the physical and the spiritual aspects of the lovers' relationship are completely interwoven with each other; the one becomes a symbol for the other, and eternity is achieved through physical union with the beloved. For the romantic, this is the existential significance of sexual experience. What is most important here, however, is not the erotic ecstasy itself, but the complete and unmediated co-presence of the one with the other that this involves. Elsewhere in *Women in Love*, for example, D. H. Lawrence describes another mode of physical presence, that calm and purposeless being with another, that promotes a similar rapture and an evocation of eternity beyond the horizon of our own selfish lives:

> She clung nearer to him. He held her close, and kissed her softly, gently. It was such peace and heavenly freedom, just to hold her and kiss her gently, and not to have any thoughts or any desires or any will, just to be still with her, to be perfectly still and together, in a peace that was not sleep, but content in bliss. To be content in bliss, without desire or insistence anywhere, this was heaven: to be together in happy stillness.[18]

In the end, the romantic desire for fusion is perhaps only the most intense expression of a deep desire for *some* kind of unity or shared identity with the beloved. And even if we are attracted by the final bliss that Tristan and Isolde achieve in their *Liebestod*, it is much more likely that we will be drawn to the possibility of a shared identity in love that transforms and inspires the two lovers without undermining their identities as separate beings. When I love someone I experience an enlargement of my own self because the loved one's desires and goals are now concerns of my own. In the deepest sense, if the one whom I love is sad or happy then I will also feel sad or happy because there is no longer a distinction in my mind between the beloved's goals and interests and my own.

On the other hand, to love someone in anything but a disinterested way involves not only desiring the beloved's happiness and well-being but also desiring that it should be oneself, and not another lover, who actually brings this about. And this desire is in opposition to the selflessness that romantic lovers usually proclaim. Hence, there may well come a point when the needs of the beloved may come into conflict with the lover's desire to strengthen their bond—when the personal ambitions of one partner seem to challenge the primacy of the romantic relation itself, or when the desire for solitude is reconstrued (perhaps inevitably) as a sign that the relationship is lacking. Jealousy, in particular, follows from a perceived threat to the shared world that I inhabit or would like to inhabit with my beloved. And it may well be that to reaffirm that world involves anger and a refusal to accept what the beloved desires. In *The Sorrows of Young Werther*, Werther is totally in love with Lotte, who is already engaged and later married to someone else. Lotte has a real affection for Werther, but eventually it becomes clear that his desire to see her and to be with her on every possible occasion is making life very difficult for her. She is anxious for her marriage and for what her husband might think, and she begs Werther to stay away while her husband is gone. But even though he promises, he visits her anyway. Lotte is right when she charges that Werther has an "uncontrollable clinging passion," which must be totally stifling.[19] And even though he later kills himself, one has the impression that he does not act for Lotte's sake, so that she can get on with her life, but for the sake of his own passion, to prove to her and to everyone else that *his* love was the most profound. "You are mine, Lotte, forever," he cries, and through his death he seeks to establish the private domain of love that he never achieved in this life.[20]

This example is instructive because it shows us how the inherent idealism of romantic love may quickly be superseded by the desire for possession and control. In *The Sorrows of Young Werther*, Goethe shows how romantic love may act as a liberating force by cutting through all of the artificial structures and conventions that normally keep people separate and isolated from each other. Through love, the self is freed from all of the received ideas and fixed responses that usually confine it. But at the same time, Goethe also shows how the anguish of romantic longing must inevitably lead to the agonies of jealousy and the simple desire to make the beloved one's own. "Sometimes," Werther exclaims, "I cannot understand how another *can*, how he *dare* love her, since I alone love her completely and devotedly, knowing only her, and having nothing in the world but her." And later he laments, "I cannot pray, 'Let her be mine!' And yet how often do I think of her as mine. I cannot pray, 'give her to me!' because she belongs to another man."[21]

In romantic love, the complete idealization of the beloved requires the projection of a real distance between the lover and the beloved. As in traditional religious attitudes, this encourages the lover's abjection and the fixing (or idolizing) of the beloved. Within such a framework, however, the desire for possession and control must prevail since this seems to be the only way of gaining access to the beloved and ensuring the continuation of the relationship in its accepted romantic form. The romantic lover, like Werther, may believe that the possession of his beloved will solve all his problems. But by focusing obsessively on the love relationship and idolizing the beloved to an impossible degree, he is able to avoid the most real and painful issues that confront him. Indeed this suggests that romantic love is not really moved by a concern for the beloved, because it is a pose and a self-preoccupation that springs from a deeper dissatisfaction with human existence and the way things are. And this in turn implies that underlying the "hopeless" passion of romantic love is a deeper yearning, namely, a desire for oblivion as the only possible solution to the problems of life.

So far, we have looked at what I would call the *inherent* problems of romantic love, or the internal contradictions within romantic love that lead to the devaluation of both lover and beloved alike. Of course, even more problems emerge once we consider the ways in which romantic love has been appropriated and used within the total economy of our culture. I do not think that romantic love is inherently sexist, but at the same time there is good reason to believe that romantic love has always functioned in a gendered way by reinforcing male and female models of subjectivity that promote the subjection of women. Contemporary feminists have argued that the model of romantic love facilitates patriarchal rule by encouraging the belief that women can only achieve personal fulfillment through their association with a man. In *The Dialectic of Sex*, Shulamith Firestone claims that "[a]s civilization advances and the biological bases of sex class crumble, male supremacy must shore itself up with artificial institutions. . . . [W]here formerly women have been held openly in contempt, now they are elevated to states of mock worship. Romanticism is a cul-

tural tool of male power to keep women from knowing their condition."[22] We do not have to accept a conspiracy theory of history
to see that there is some truth in this claim. Particularly when
romantic love is held to require an unconditional sacrifice and
devotion, and when (male) thinkers claim that a woman's nature is
to love, the result is that women often sacrifice any possibility of
personal fulfillment for the requirements of love and completion
through the beloved.

Simone de Beauvoir has pointed out that the ideal of romantic
love confirms a woman's status as a secondary being to another
(the man), who is actively encouraged to seek fulfillment in his
own career and in other areas of personal achievement. "The fact
is," she writes,

> that we have nothing to do here with laws of nature. It is the differ-
> ence in their situations that is reflected in the difference men and
> women show in their conceptions of love. The individual who is a
> subject, who is himself, if he has the courageous inclination towards
> transcendence, endeavours to extend his grasp on the world; he is
> ambitious, he acts. But an inessential creature is incapable of sens-
> ing the absolute at the heart of her subjectivity; a being doomed to
> immanence cannot find self-realization in acts. Shut up in the
> sphere of the relative, destined to the male from childhood, habitu-
> ated to seeing in him a superb being whom she cannot possibly
> equal, the woman who has not repressed her claim to humanity will
> dream of transcending her being toward one of these superior
> beings, of amalgamating herself with the sovereign subject. There is
> no other way out for her than to lose herself, body and soul, in him
> who is represented to her as the absolute, as the essential.

She adds,

> She chooses to desire her enslavement so ardently that it will seem
> to her the expression of her liberty; she will try to rise above her sit-
> uation as inessential object by fully accepting it; through her flesh,
> her feelings, her behavior, she will enthrone him as supreme value
> and reality: she will humble herself to nothingness before him. Love
> becomes for her a religion.[23]

Romantic love has remained especially important to women
because it is historically one of the few areas of life in which
women have been offered the possibility of personal fulfillment,
apparently on the same terms as men. Given this situation, women
have become "specialists" in love and have come to embrace the

intimacy and emotional skills that have devolved to them as an essential part of their nature. But as both de Beauvoir and Firestone point out, romantic love actually promotes the economic and emotional dependency of women by requiring the sacrifice of most other aspirations. However it may function in any particular case, in global terms the net effect of romantic love is to reinforce the submission of women by encouraging them to seek personal fulfillment through a private love relationship as the substitute for self-actualization in the world.

Romantic love is often presented as the locus of self-understanding and fulfillment. We are often told that "all you need is love," and it sometimes seems that the most important project is to find somebody to love in a romantic way. In this respect, the ideal of romantic love also requires self-suppression and sacrifice for the sake of a personal destiny that, it is held, can only be fulfilled by coming together with another who is able to complete one's own partial nature as a woman or a man. Traditionally, romantic love binds women to the home and the family and reinforces their position as the mediators of everyday personal life. By contrast, the model of complementarity that underlies romantic love tends toward the psychical disfigurement of men and what is often perceived as their comparative "inadequacy" in the sphere of personal intimacy.

From all of this, we might conclude that romantic love has been used as a tool of subjection, but that given a different political order, or even very enlightened individuals, romantic love could one day become a means of mutual enhancement and fulfillment. So should we try to rehabilitate romantic love as it exists and remove it from its present oppressive context, or should we now think of alternatives to romantic love that would celebrate the intimate encounter between two separate human beings? It would be a false abstraction to consider a given feature of our present society in total isolation from all of the forces that condition and maintain it. But insofar as it is possible to talk about romantic love in general, I think it is now clear that the latter requires us to think of ourselves as partial beings who are inherently lacking. From this perspective, no amount of personal striving will ever satisfy my basic dissatisfaction and yearning, and I can only experience fulfillment through the mediation of another who confers value on me by establishing a particular kind of relationship with me. In no way do I want to deny that the basic human reality is one of complete interdependence, and I do not want to argue that autonomy is possible by withdrawing from other people. My point is simply that the total fulfillment of one's human nature as a reasonable and spiritual, physical and emotional creature, as an active individual and as a nurturing caregiver becomes impossible as long as one follows this particular romantic model.

It may be argued, then, that at the world-historical level, romantic love is a ruling idea that serves the obvious interests of the dominant (male) class. At the level of the individual psyche, romantic love must always encourage possessiveness and control, because taking the specific other as the locus of personal fulfillment requires me to think of the other in possessive terms as "mine" or as my own property, if not as an extension of myself. The continual danger of loss makes the continued possession of the other something that is fraught with difficulty and pain. In short, romantic love *requires* us to view the appropriation of the other as the completion of the self and as the final achievement of self-respect, and it is therefore self-regarding love in this sense.

But what about a passionate love that presupposes an integral selfhood and self-respect or which fosters their achievement while eschewing the ordinary path of domination and control? A love that truly values the other person while it also avoids the traditional religious impulse to exalt the beloved or to frame the relationship within the religious horizon of eternity? Whatever else we may be able to say about it, such a nonappropriative and human love suggests an alternative to romantic love as it is commonly considered, and it is to this possibility that we must now turn.

The Possibility of Postromantic Love

Many of our expectations in life are created and sustained by ruling paradigms and ideals that effectively condition our thinking in advance. For the past two hundred years, romantic love has been the paradigm of passionate encounter between two individuals, and romantic fulfillment is now regarded as an indispensable condition for personal happiness. The problem is that for many people romantic experience is often unhappy; even the ideal lovers— Romeo and Juliet, Tristan and Isolde, or Cathy and Heathcliff—are frequently made wretched and miserable by their love, if they live long enough to experience it. A typical response is to condemn ourselves and to think that there must be something wrong with us if we cannot achieve the romantic ideal. But of course, it would be just as reasonable to challenge the paradigm itself as an excessive, if not an impossible, goal that distorts all our thinking and leads us inevitably to a miserable conclusion.

So far, I have argued that romantic love is a quasi-religious ideal that cultivates religious attitudes of devotion and yearning and projects salvation through the beloved. In this respect, the ideal goal of romantic love is fusion or some kind of a shared identity that would mark the overcoming of individual isolation and despair and the achievement of "eternity" through the beloved. Romantic lovers inhabit their own world, and although this does not need to entail the suppression of separate interests or to involve doing everything together, their individual identity is to a great extent superseded by the formation of this "we self." According to the romantic model, only the latter brings fulfillment and completion to the individual life.

Similar to this, in marriage two people present a united front to the world. In sharing a household or raising children together they will usually retain different interests and ideas, and may often be in conflict with each other. But there is also a sense in which they have committed themselves to each other by joining together in a common project that sometimes requires them to sacrifice their own personal desires for the sake of that shared identity. An example is the spouse who decides to sacrifice her career for the sake of her marriage, although she may not even view it as a "sacrifice" at all. In *To the Lighthouse*, Virginia Woolf describes the very moment when such a relationship suddenly becomes articulate and known:

> She knew from the effort, the rise in his voice to surmount a difficult word that it was the first time he had said "we." "We did this, we did that." They'll say that all their lives, she thought . . . a curious sense rising in her, at once freakish and tender, of celebrating a festival, as if two emotions were called up in her, one profound—for what could be more serious than the love of man for woman, what more commanding, more impressive, bearing in its bosom the seeds of death; at the same time these lovers, these people entering into illusion glittering eyed, must be danced round with mockery, decorated with garlands.[24]

Here, the romantic couple is both respected and mocked. The lovers are bound to take themselves seriously, and their shared intimacy is supposed to transfigure their lives. But from another, external, perspective their romantic project is also a bit ridiculous and is a futile attempt to shelter themselves from the reality of the world.

The question now is, What, if anything, is the nature of that common project that should arise within passionate love? And is it possible to describe the essential contours of this kind of intimacy? The response will allow us to reflect more clearly on the shared identity, or "we self," that is specifically aimed for by lovers. Earlier, I argued that in erotic love we are allowed the most intense and passionate experience of another person. In the stirring of erotic desire we are abruptly jolted out of our everyday perceptions and awareness, and through the transfiguration of the beloved we begin to experience everything with renewed clarity and depth. It is in this sense that passionate love unfixes the individual subject from all of its previous encrustations and engenders the self-in-process that is capable of so much empowerment and depth because it is now open to new perceptions and to all of the energies of life. In this respect, passionate love should be a mutually transformative encounter; and if it is to continue, it must be reciprocal, for the self-in-process can only be evoked and sustained by another that is like it. In the shared project of passionate love, two people are engaged in the mutual goal of self-transformation, continually stimulating and inspiring each other to discover new strengths and powers and to become more than they have been hitherto. This is the spiritual corollary of the physical passion that binds them both.

The model of passionate love that I am describing obviously involves mutual respect and a profound acknowledgment of the beloved's own autonomy and difference. In fact, it seems to require a degree of separation and distance between the two lovers in order to preserve and enhance the personal sovereignty of each of them. Such an emphasis would not be problematic if we were dealing with friendship, for the latter relationship is based on the mutual recognition of two independent beings whose care and concern for each other is all the more valuable since it is freely given and does not obviously arise from any kind of physical or biological necessity. Erotic desire, on the other hand, is a form of compulsion. And it is completely spontaneous in the sense that it is not constrained by the will. As the romantics recognized, erotic passion must involve self-abandonment, and the passionate love that is driven by erotic desire is characterized by the blurring of the boundaries between self and other, whether this is experienced in sexual union or in romantic passion itself. "I cannot express it," Catherine declares in *Wuthering Heights*,

> but surely you and everybody have a notion that there is or should be
> an existence of yours beyond you. What were the use of my creation,

if I were entirely contained here? My great miseries in this world have been Heathcliff's miseries, and I watched and felt each from the beginning: my great thought in living is himself. If all else perished and *he* remained, I should still continue to be and if all else remained and he were annihilated, the universe would turn to a mighty stranger. I should not seem part of it. . . . Nelly, I *am* Heathcliff. He's always, always in my mind—not as a pleasure, anymore than I am always a pleasure to myself—but as my own being.[25]

This passage is so powerful because it affirms the value of passionate love in escaping from the limited horizons of the self and in the absolute and unconditional identification with another person. Of course, an even stronger example would be Heathcliff's love for Cathy, for while she is sometimes afraid of this passionate love and even tries to escape it by marrying the sensible Linton, Heathcliff does everything he can to assert and intensify their emotional bond to each other. He refuses to accept that she has married someone else, and he torments her because of this, even affirming their passion through the workings of his revenge after she is dead. I do not want to endorse such a perspective, but it serves to emphasize the problem that we may lose everything that is important and distinctive about passionate love if we insist on the distance that is implied by respect and the recognition of individual autonomy. Indeed, to assimilate passionate love to the model of friendship in this way is effectively to destroy it *as* passionate love.

As we have seen, however, the excesses of romantic love move in the other direction. Romantic love celebrates fusion and the merging of two separate identities into a blissful "oneness" of soul. In this respect, it valorizes self-abandonment and allows one to avoid the difficult requirements of personal sovereignty by affirming one's own passion as the most important thing. Romantic love becomes geared toward the physical or emotional possession of the beloved. But at this point, or even before it, the self-transformation that the lover undergoes will end. Romantic love reaches such an impasse because it requires the complete subordination of personal autonomy to the requirements of the relationship itself. Indeed, any significant desire, like the desire for solitude, that is not somehow subsumed or validated by romantic union may be regarded as a betrayal and the sign of an insufficient love.

What all of this shows, then, is that passionate love actually requires both moments of separation and unity if it is to flourish. Even though these two poles may at first appear to be completely at odds with each other, they are actually supporting conditions that intensify and motivate each other through the very tension that exists between them. Passionate love requires a relationship that grants a periodic satisfaction to both the claims of autonomy and mutuality. And to sustain their relationship the lovers must actively reflect on the terms of their involvement with each other, lest they succumb to a conventional model of partnership that obliterates either one of these two defining poles. In passionate love, both principles must be honored, not because these are separate needs that must both be attended to, but because autonomy and mutuality actually serve to enhance each other. In any amatory encounter, the experience of being totally connected and at one with another person is so powerful and even astonishing because it *is* the experience of another person, who is not encountered merely as an object in my perceptual field but as an embodied subject who remains different from me. Likewise, the lover's autonomy and individual achievement is actually supported by the strong acceptance and endorsement that he or she receives from the security of the love relationship itself. There is no final contradiction between autonomy and unity—only an ongoing tension that requires both lovers to balance and negotiate these claims in an ongoing way. Perhaps the requirements of autonomy may lead the lovers to live apart, or, if they have less in common and come from different backgrounds, they may work on a common project that would require their sustained cooperation and community with each other. At a certain point, passionate love may involve taking a risk and accepting the other's choice as that which is best for nurturing the relationship. Or it may require a principled stand and a refusal to compromise if the individual believes that not to do so would smother the individual life.

None of this is meant to offer any kind of a blueprint for the various forms that passionate love might take. Indeed, one of the biggest problems with romantic love is that it is so highly structured and organized in advance, even down to the very phrases that lovers repeat to each other. In this respect, it easily constrains and even destroys the individual life that should be nurtured by it. In his writings, as well as in his own life, the poet Rilke was very much aware of the way in which the ruling paradigm of love can restrict the relationship between two individuals:

> And so each of them loses himself for the sake of the other person, and loses the other, and many others who still wanted to come. And loses the vast distances and possibilities, gives up the approaching

and fleeing of gentle, prescient Things in exchange for an unfruitful
confusion, out of which nothing more can come; nothing but a bit of
disgust, disappointment and poverty, and the escape into one of the
many conventions that have been put up in great numbers like public shelters on this most dangerous road.[26]

Rilke also understood that to live outside of the ruling paradigms
requires an exceptional courage but this may finally be rewarded
by the depth of experience that is thereby revealed. For in chal-
lenging the romantic ideal, we open up a wholly new space for
personal encounter that must be appropriated by the individuals
involved. And as the ordinary and accepted forms of romantic
response are regarded as more plainly problematic, individuals are
empowered insofar as they must consciously and deliberately create the relational structures that they choose to inhabit.

Among recent philosophers, there is still, I think, a tendency to
ignore the reality of passionate love or to view it as a secondary
realm that lacks an intrinsic importance of its own. An important
exception, however, is Luce Irigaray, who views the domain of
erotic encounter and sexual difference in particular as the most
productive and important field both for philosophy and for the
future of humankind.[27] In fact, much of Irigaray's work is an
attempt to rethink the amorous exchange and to articulate the
forms of erotic encounter when these are not encumbered and
appropriated by "duty," which tends to destroy love. How does
love between two individuals become a productive and enabling
force that promotes the real sovereignty of both? And on the other
hand, how does it lead to self-abandonment and the appropriation
of the other in a relationship that is basically one of conflict? Discussion of Irigaray's work may help us to clarify the authentic
forms of passionate love.

According to Irigaray, it is perhaps an inevitable corollary of
men's economic and political domination that their control of public life will be reinscribed on the interpersonal level. This gives rise
to two different approaches to love that roughly correspond to the
typically male and the (ideal) female form of passionate encounter.
As Irigaray writes, "Love can be the becoming which appropriates
the other for itself by consuming it, introjecting it into itself, to the
point where the other disappears. Or love can be the motor of
becoming, allowing both the one and the other to grow. For such a
love, each must keep their body autonomous. The one should not
be the source of the other nor the other of the one. Two lives should
embrace and fertilise each other, without either being a fixed goal

for the other."[28] The masculine urge, if we can call it that, is toward appropriation and control, and whether we are talking about philosophy or romance it is that which always tends toward the reduction and the confinement of the other—in the home or in the system—in such a way that the possibility of an open and ongoing dynamic between self and other is forever lost. In this context, romantic relationships must follow the logic of master-slave relations that Hegel describes elsewhere. Indeed, the independence and subjectivity of the other is an objection and an affront to the self that must be annulled. Such a relationship thereby destroys the possibility of mutual empowerment and growth that Irigaray describes in the second part of this passage.

In other contexts, Irigaray recalls that the passion of wonder is often projected as the original impulse to philosophy; presumably, it is also "wonder" concerning the other that must be maintained if the spiritual possibilities of a relationship between two individuals are to thrive. But appropriation and objectification entail the end of wonder. Once the forms of our encounter are fixed, nothing new can ever happen between us. Wonder implies a full bestowal of attention and care that allows the other to be exactly who he or she is. It implies a nonappropriative relationship in which I am ready to nurture and care for someone who is also the subject of a life, without projecting my own desires and needs upon him or her.

In this respect, then, Irigaray shows how love, as distinct from obsession, must cultivate the autonomy of the other as the very condition for its own fecundity and continued existence. Irigaray finds an analogue for this form of nonappropriative encounter in the physical reality of the female body:

> Your skin and mine, yes. But mine goes on touching itself indefinitely, from the inside. Secreting a flow which brings the sides together. From which side does that liquid come? One or the other? Both? So which is one and which is other in that production? Neither? Yet it exists. Where does it come from? From both. It flows between. Not held or held back by a source. The source already rises from the two caressing.[29]

If philosophy and our amorous relations are historically dominated by male metaphors of penetration and by phallocentrism in general, then the first and most crucial step in reversing this bias would be to privilege another (female) metaphor that also suggests an alternative ideal for the amorous relationship. "Is it necessary," she continues, "to come out of that flowing between the two touching each other? Why should the solidity of an erection be more valuable than the fluidity of a flow between two?"[30]

Irigaray is not an essentialist. But given the way in which public and private life is historically organized, typically "male" and "female" approaches to love do exist, and Irigaray describes the tension between them. The difference between male and female has been ignored, reified, and mythologized, but it still functions as the most provocative difference that continues to inspire and enhance the forms of romantic life, resisting every attempt to reduce it and explain it. "Not in me," she writes, "but in our difference lies the abyss. We can never be sure of bridging the gap between us. But that is our adventure. Without this peril there is no us. If you turn it into a guarantee, you separate us."[31] Throughout her work, Irigaray tries to rethink the possibility of erotic or romantic love, and in this passage she clearly rejects the traditional romantic ideal of fusion or merger with the beloved, which implies self-abandonment and the erosion of a productive difference between two subjects that could inspire their continuing encounter.

As we have seen, Irigaray perceives an analogy between the biological difference of men and women and the appropriative and nonappropriative forms of love. This attempt to conflate the physical with the spiritual is an essential part of her project. The physical is only debased if it is contrasted or opposed to that which is purely spiritual, while the "spiritual" becomes impossible or irrelevant if it bears no relation, or only an antagonistic one, to the body itself. Erotic love is problematic because it is a domain of experience that cannot be reduced, without falsification, to a physical explanation or to a purely spiritual one. Erotic love, as opposed to lust, is the physical expression of a spiritual longing, and an idealizing projection that is nonetheless rooted in physical desire. The irreducibility of love to the carnal *or* the spiritual hints at the falsity of traditional philosophical distinctions. In Irigaray's case it inspires an appreciation for Asian philosophy and in particular yoga, which espouses the spiritualization of the body. As she comments elsewhere:

> In these [Asian] traditions, the body is cultivated to become both more spiritual and more carnal at the same time. A range of movements and nutritional practices, attentiveness to breath in respiration, respect for the rhythms of day and night, for the seasons and years as the calendar of the flesh, for the world and for history, the training of the senses for accurate, rewarding and concentrated per-

ception—all these gradually bring the body to rebirth, to give birth to itself, carnally and spiritually, at each moment of every day. The body is thus no longer simply a body engendered by my parents; it is also the one I give back to myself. Likewise, immortality is no longer reserved for the beyond and the conditions for it cease to be determined by one who is other to me. Each woman and each man acquires immortality by respecting life and its spiritualization.[32]

As a philosopher, Irigaray follows Nietzsche's advice to reject otherworldly hopes and to remain faithful to the earth—and this she achieves through a profound sense of the spiritual significance of erotic life.

This discussion helps us to understand that love and proper autonomy are not mutually exclusive, and that love as a principle of individual development and growth actually requires something like the projected sovereignty of each individual as the condition for its fulfillment. What is fundamental for human beings is not their self-involvement or their success in controlling others, but their affirmative connection and involvement with each other. For it is the latter that provides us with the possibility of personal development, and through the love of another such personal growth may be enhanced to the highest degree. Thus, in a profound sense the possibility of autonomy is really founded on the nonoppositional encounter with another person that has already been described. In this respect, the amorous relationship is especially significant because it is spiritual, emotional, and physical and testifies to the development of the whole person. The example of Irigaray shows, finally, how in becoming conscious of the limitations of romantic love we may also become much more aware of the sacred dimension of life—not the sacred in the sense of an otherworldly beyond to which we are briefly drawn in the highest moments of passion, but the sacred as the astonishing depth and significance of individuals and of the world that lies beneath the routine and ordinary aspect of things that typically confronts us.

The Future of Romantic Love

When a ruling paradigm begins to break down, life becomes much more uncertain because the accepted or traditional forms of response can no longer be viewed as necessary or natural. At this point, however, it becomes possible to think more clearly about alternative models of human relationship and to challenge the prevailing patterns of belief. So far, I have emphasized the internal problems of romantic love and the respect in which it constrains

the individual life by undermining the possibility of authentic relations with another person. But quite apart from these inner difficulties, we have also seen that romantic love is a historically
conditioned phenomenon. There are now good reasons for believ-
ing that it must eventually decline as a relevant and compelling
ideal. We can briefly consider two of these reasons before we conclude with a final estimation of the value of romantic love.

First, and most important, is the rise in the position of women in
recent years—their economic and educational advancement—
which contributes to the increasing democratization of modern
life. In the past, the traditional ideal of romantic love has helped to
ensure the continued subjection of women by requiring a total sacrifice of everything for the beloved. In the context of an uneven
and unjust division of labor, this has actually meant that women
were required to sacrifice their own individual needs to become
the domestic and emotional caretakers of men, who were able to
go out and provide. Hence the final ambivalence concerning
romantic love that many women feel, and which Virginia Woolf
expresses through a female character who is attracted and yet
repelled by the exigency of romantic love:

> Yet she said to herself, from the dawn of time odes have been sung
> to love; wreaths have been heaped and roses; and if you asked nine
> people out of ten they would say they wanted nothing but this—
> love; while the women judging from their own experience would all
> the time be feeling, This is not what we want; there is nothing more
> tedious, puerile and inhumane than this; yet it is also beautiful and
> necessary.[33]

As a woman achieves more personal and economic autonomy,
however, she will also be less constrained to find a man who will
provide for her. She will no longer be forced to regard success in
life and personal fulfillment as things that can only occur through
romantic identification with a man. As a result, the relationship
between men and women, or any two lovers, will increasingly
become something that is chosen and affirmed by the individuals
involved simply because it is an inherently good thing—and not
for the sake of economic security, or respectability, or sexual satisfaction that would otherwise be unavailable. Such a relationship
will last for as long as the individuals decide that they want it to; in
this context, love will no longer be destroyed by becoming a duty.
Thus, de Beauvoir writes about the future possibilities of passionate love, arguing, indeed, that the true emancipation of women

requires a new version of romantic experience: "Genuine love ought to be founded on the mutual recognition of two liberties. [T]he lovers would then experience themselves both as self and as other: neither would give up transcendence, neither would be mutilated; together they would manifest values and aims in the world. For the one and the other, love would be revelation of self by the gift of self and enrichment of the world." She continues:

> On the day when it will be possible for woman to love not in her weakness but in her strength, not to escape herself but to find herself, not to abase herself but to assert herself—on that day love will become for her, as for man, a source of life and not of mortal danger. In the meantime, love represents in its most touching form the curse that lies heavily upon woman confined in the feminine universe, woman mutilated, insufficient to herself. The innumerable martyrs to love bear witness against the injustice of a fate that offers a sterile hell as ultimate salvation.[34]

Beauvoir, like many others, has argued that romantic love is a ruling idea that serves the interests of the dominant male class. But as more and more economic and educational opportunities become available to women, we are also more likely to see the emergence of a nonappropriative love that is based on desire and mutual concern and whose goal is not fulfillment through the other (as in romantic love) but fulfillment of self and other through their reciprocal enhancement.

The second point is more speculative. The conceptual analysis of romantic love is finally inseparable from the historical genealogy that describes its most decisive moments. Although the romantic ideal can be found in both ancient and medieval texts, it would be true to say that romantic love first became a dominant and a popular theme with the birth of the modern age and the rise of the bourgeois subject. Since about the middle of the eighteenth century, the self-contained and self-sufficient individual has been both a popular and a philosophical ideal; at the same time, in opposition to all the perceived requirements of individual subjectivity, romantic love has always suggested the countervailing possibility of self-abandonment and escape. Thus the modern age brings with it the imperative of autonomy and the absolute requirement that we should take charge of our lives. It intensifies individual responsibility and self-determination. But it also sees an explosion in the popular themes of romantic love, celebrating excessive passion, self-surrender, and fusion with the beloved.

Given their emergence together, it does not seem unreasonable to regard these ideas as correlated, with romantic love as the negative image of autonomy within the total economy of thought.

Paralleling this conceptual development, and certainly related to it, is the strong division between the public and the private spheres of life that also characterizes the modern age. Romantic love exists in the private domain, and it also exists primarily for those individuals—women—who are historically bound to it. Perhaps we should say that in romantic love, a woman achieves an imaginary identification with the phantom of a strong, self-sufficient (male) subject when society has denied her the occupation and financial independence that are the material conditions for achieving this directly for herself. Conversely, in romantic love a man achieves some release from the oppressive structures of subjectivity. What seems clear is that autonomy and love reciprocally imply and evoke each other at several levels, and the understanding of the one is really incomplete without the understanding of the other.

Is the modern age finally over? Is there still a strong requirement to be a sovereign subject? Or has the very nature of our experience and our relationship to ourselves changed? If it has, and this is what I argue in conclusion, then traditional romantic love has no future and we must look for other models in order to understand, if not evoke, new forms of human encounter and relationship that would not be ordered by nostalgia for this vanishing ideal.

To show that romantic love as we know it has no future would require nothing less than a massive phenomenology of contemporary experience, which would make it clear that the model of the autonomous subject has diminished as a ruling ideal. Certainly, at the philosophical level, the very idea of the subject as a self-enthroned ego and creator of its own law has been challenged by the whole tendency of recent thought. Foucault, Heidegger, Derrida, and before them Marx, Freud, and Nietzsche all point to the respect in which the subjectivity of the subject is a construction or even an illusion. To understand ourselves we must first understand the libidinal and economic forces that subtend and support us, the very language that precedes us and discloses our world to us, and the arrangements of power that organize us *as subjects* in the first place.

But the death of the subject in recent philosophy is only a symptom on the intellectual plane of something that is happening at the most basic level of experience as we move from the modern into the postmodern world. To be a subject today does *not* involve thinking of oneself as an autonomous and self-sufficient agent. More than ever, it means to understand oneself as the nexus and embodiment of particular histories and particular interests that put one into shifting and mobile alliances with particular groups and others—to be a woman, for example, and to be pro-life; to be black and to be middle class; to be Jewish and to be gay; to work for the environment and to draw a salary from IBM; to be a single parent and to be a born-again Christian; to be a student or unemployed. Such complex affiliations determine our existence and our understanding of ourselves. Whereas in the past, romantic love offered the possibility of transcendence from the universal requirements of autonomy, or the illusory achievement of self-sufficiency itself, today it is no longer so relevant.

Romantic love is a mediated relationship of the self to itself by means of the other. What has changed in contemporary experience is that with the erosion of autonomy—both as a fact and as an ideal—such a mediation is no longer necessary. Now the self encounters itself more directly, regarding every claim to transcendence, including romantic love, with cynicism and ironic detachment. Similarly, the possibility of romantic love recedes as this inherent *narcissism* becomes a prevailing feature of contemporary life. "Narcissism" suggests self-immersion and self-preoccupation, such that everything that we encounter—nature, the world, other people—is just a possibility for self-gratification and the accumulation of interesting experiences. But narcissism is not simply equivalent to excessive selfishness. In fact, the narcissist is one who fails to make clear the distinction between himself and everything else; he is *not* preoccupied with the illusions of autonomy and self-mastery, because he no longer has any strong sense of his distinction and separation from the rest of the world.[35] Thus, as reflected by recent philosophy, the contemporary experience is one of a *lack* of self, where the individual finds herself plugged into various systems of images, machines, and experiences. The goal now is not to encounter and process reality, but simply to cope with it while deriving whatever satisfactions one can; and in such a context, the ideal forms of autonomy and romantic love will be cynically regarded.

Perhaps this state of affairs can be explained by the logic of late capitalism; perhaps it is the final consequence of consumerism and the construction of a self that is made to define itself exclusively in terms of its own wants and needs. In any case, *romantic* love is now contradicted and opposed by another version of the self-preoccupation that created it in the first place. But the decline of romantic love, and related forms such as marriage and the traditional family, should force us to come to grips with more authentic forms of interpersonal encounters that acknowledge both our separation and our interdependence. Through the cultivation of this space, a sense of the meaningful character of human existence may be restored.

Love, especially passionate love, is absolutely important and valuable insofar as it discloses the sacred character of the world and transfigures our own experience. In love, I cherish the other person; indeed, I experience the latter as the subject of his or her own life, which is much more than just to recognize that he or she is self-determining. In this respect, the boundaries of my own self-concern are loosened and enlarged. In many ways, passionate love offers the most abrupt and powerful possibilities of self-transformation, since it charges the physical, emotional, and spiritual aspects of the individual life. It is the most intense and urgent experience of love and allows both lovers to flourish in the encounter with each other. But even though it belongs to the morphology of passionate love, romantic love encourages religious postures of abjection and self-abandonment and projects the emotional and physical possession of the beloved as the final goal of romantic fulfillment. In this way it misses the unique reality of the other person and constrains passion by fixing the relationship between the two lovers within the highly scripted and organized space of the romantic encounter. For all these reasons, we may now look forward to the end of romantic love and the emergence of postromantic possibilities that are reflectively sustained.

3

From Parents to Children

A mother's love is supposed to be the most unconditional of all loves. Indeed, it is often viewed as the inevitable expression of a natural instinct that even nonhuman species possess. Thus female apes, cats, and dogs are all supposed to protect and nurture their young. But their love is not a matter of preference or choice; because it is biologically driven, it is automatic and innate. Hence it is sometimes said that the experience of motherhood represents the natural fulfillment of every woman's life, whereas if a woman neglects or abuses her own children she is viewed as an unnatural creature. All of this may seem unremarkable. A mother carries her child within herself from the moment of conception until the moment of birth, and usually she continues to love and nurture her child in every possible way for many years afterward. Even when her child is fully grown, her maternal feelings of protection and caring will probably remain. What stronger evidence could there be for the existence of a natural maternal instinct? And yet this may not be a purely biological response, for what we call a mother's love may actually be a response that is evoked by a specific situation. Thus, it would be hard to deny that adoptive mothers experience the same intense feelings for their nonbiological children. Similarly, if a man is actively involved in raising and nurturing a child, it is not clear that his emotional capacities and feelings are appreciably different or diminished in comparison to those of a woman.

Given all of this, however, we may still want to insist that there is no more intense relationship than the one that exists between parents and children, for whether a parent's love is innate or the conditioned response to a being who needs nurturance and protection, it is still a wholly powerful passion that can be measured by the sacrifices that parents are prepared to make on an everyday and continuing basis. Or could it be the case that even this much is historically contingent? In 1960, the French historian Philippe Aries published his classic work *Centuries of Childhood,* in which he argued that the concept of childhood really did not exist in the Middle Ages. "This is not to suggest that children were neglected, forsaken or despised," he writes. "The idea of childhood is not to be confused with affection for children: it corresponds to an awareness of the particular nature of childhood, that particular nature which distinguishes the child from the adult. . . . In medieval society, this awareness was lacking."[1] According to Aries, there were no clothes or games that were designed especially for children in the medieval period. Children were allowed to play games of chance that we might consider appropriate only for an adult. There was not any strong sense that children had to be carefully nurtured and protected from the adult world, and in the art of the time children are typically depicted as if they were miniature adults. As soon as children were weaned (usually between the ages of three and five) and deemed capable of living without a nurse or mother, they became participating members of adult society. Aries claims that it is only in the seventeenth century that two concepts of childhood gradually emerge. According to the first of these, childhood was a natural state of sin and evil, and no effort was to be spared in bringing children to a sense of their need for salvation. According to the other way of thinking, children were amusing creatures who should be coddled and doted on.

Aries's claims have been disputed. He relies almost exclusively on French sources, and he fails to note that there were some fields, such as medicine, where the specificity of childhood was definitely understood. But what is important for us is Aries's claim that "childhood" is not a natural given. There is plenty of evidence to support the point that childhood is a social construction that changes from one age to the next. Thus, St. Augustine's casual comments about children and the wickedness of the crying infant are problematic today because they are totally at odds with our modern sensibilities. In the *Confessions,* he asks: "Is it not a sin to lust after the breast and wail, for if I now lust with similar ardor after a food appropriate to my age, people would ridicule me. . . . It is therefore an evil desire since in growing up we tear it out and cast it aside."[2] In the nineteenth century, this negative view of childhood as an inferior sinful state still existed: Edmund Gosse's description of his own Victorian childhood in *Father and Son* is an obvious case in point.[3] But with Rousseau and later the Romantics there emerged a cult of the child as a naturally pure and good being. Blake and Wordsworth, in particular, celebrated the innocence and the goodness of childhood. The child was supposed to have a natural attunement to nature and a spontaneous joy that was gradually stifled by the corruptions of adult life. The Romantic task was accordingly to preserve and integrate the qualities of childhood within the mature individual's life. Later, in the Victorian age, the romantic celebration of childhood deteriorated into sentimentality. In Dickens especially, the figure of the innocent child—Little Nell, Little Dorrit, or Oliver Twist—was used to highlight the inhumanity of the society of adults.

In the present age, a tremendous amount is now being written and reported on the nature of childhood by professionals and childcare experts, and yet it must be noted that there is still disagreement over most topics: whether it is ever right to hit a child, whether it is healthy to allow a toddler to continue breast-feeding or to share a bed with his or her parents, or whether daycare or divorce is in the best interests of the child. In fact, the whole domain of childhood has become heavily circumscribed by "experts," and all the issues of child rearing and child development are currently areas of intense anxiety and concern.

The point of this review is that if there is a history in the various conceptions of childhood, then presumably the ways in which parents relate to their children, their feelings toward their children, and the forms of parental love will also vary from one age to the next. Therefore, it will become much harder to postulate an underlying "mother love," or a parental love of any kind, that remains the same throughout history.

In the past, it has been customary to distinguish a mother's love from a father's love as if these were eternal archetypes.[4] A mother's love is said to be unconditional. It cannot be acquired or lost since it involves an attitude of pure acceptance and complete generosity toward the child that the latter does not need to earn or even reciprocate. In this sense, a mother's love is absolute and she is capable of any sacrifice—physical, emotional, or even moral—for the sake of her child. Wherever such a love exists it becomes the basis for the child's own self-esteem and future ability to love. The only danger is that since a mother's love is so soft and yielding, it is also indulgent; according to our received ideas, the child who is smothered with such love will remain fixed at this point of emotional development, unable to grow up and forever dependent on another. By contrast, however, a father's love is held to be much stricter and more conditional in nature. The father is supposed to be the one who teaches the child and shows him the way into the world. His task is to make the child autonomous and morally secure, and so his love may be withheld if the child does not fulfill the father's expectations. The Roman Gaius Manlius is often portrayed as the pure embodiment of the paternal principle. He executed his own son because the latter disobeyed the general order not to fight, even though by so doing he defeated the Etruscans.[5]

Prescriptive ideals such as these serve to shape and condition all of our thinking and all of our behavior as mothers and fathers. But this means that we often condemn ourselves if we cannot live up to the image that they propose. Thus a mother may find herself angry and annoyed at her children or her situation in general, and so she becomes even angrier with herself, and full of self-loathing, because she cannot live up to the received image of motherhood as a state of intense peacefulness and calm. As Adrienne Rich puts it: "Love and anger *can* exist concurrently; anger at the conditions of motherhood can become translated into anger at the child, along with the fear that we are not 'loving'; grief at all we cannot do for our children in a society so inadequate to meet human needs becomes translated into guilt and self-laceration."[6] Likewise, a father may find it impossible and even repellent to maintain the strict and inflexible discipline that is apparently required of fatherhood in general. A father is supposed to be the representative of the law; it is thought that he betrays himself as well as his children if he allows his rules and principles to follow the lead of his current emotional state. But in what sense are these images of parental love even remotely accurate or essential from a historical or cross-cultural perspective? And more important, do they illuminate the highest possibilities of love between parents and children, or do they simply propose a limited and distorted ideal? As we have seen, when a ruling image is found to be at odds with our own experience of the world, we can either condemn ourselves for failing to live up to the ideal or we can abandon the ideal itself, since it is unhelpful and does not correspond to the way things are.

Let us briefly consider just one historical episode that will help to illustrate the contingency of parental love as a historical form. According to Elizabeth Badinter's research, in 1780, before Rousseau's ideas about children had become popular, 21,000 infants were born in Paris.[7] Of these, 19,000 were sent out of

Paris and into the country to be nursed by other women. Partly because of the appalling conditions that these children had to endure, more than half of them died before the age of two. The practice of wet-nursing had been popular for centuries, and throughout Europe it was a common practice for the wealthiest parents as well as for those who were themselves poor. Often a mother would not even see her child before it had been weaned. As Badinter remarks, when there was great sorrow for children who died, it was usually noted because this was something exceptional rather than the rule. In this context, she quotes Montaigne's famous comments from two centuries before: "I lost three children during their stay with the wet nurse—not without regret, mind you, but without any great vexation."[8]

Should we see this as a sign of emotional self-protection on the part of the parents? Times were hard, and given that so many children were bound to die anyway, perhaps it was best not to have them around until they had survived the perils of infancy. But it is more complicated than this, because it was probably the conditions in these nursing mills that killed a lot of children who would not otherwise have died. To say that parents were practicing emotional self-protection when they farmed their children out to strangers is really begging the question. It assumes that there must be an underlying parental impulse that sometimes has to be denied for one's own good. Perhaps it would be more realistic to say that during this period, and for whatever reason, parents simply did not care as much for their children. To argue that this may be explained by harsh economic circumstances is certainly feasible, for it would explain how the cult of the child became more popular once the economic situation had improved in postrevolutionary times. But this would be to accept that maternal love, and parental love in general, is not absolute and unchanging but is subject to external conditions and forces, and is even occasionally absent.

Likewise, the traditional opposition between motherly love and paternal love is especially unhelpful when many children are nurtured and raised by a single parent, or when care of the home and being a provider are not divided along traditional male-female lines. The opposition between maternal and paternal love is a false opposition, and if our goal is to nurture a child in the most loving way, we will have to construct another model of parental love that includes the strengths traditionally attributed both to mothers and to fathers. Parental love, like friendship and romantic love, is a historical formation that has taken different shapes over the centuries. But to accept this is not to deny that there can be better or worse forms of parental love. There are obviously both good and bad parents, which suggests that our own contemporary ideal of parental love is also subject to an ethical transformation. In this book, I have assumed that each form of love makes implicit reference to its own ideal, and that we get closer to the truth of friendship, for example, once we examine its ancient and modern versions and the differences and deficiencies of each of these. But in this regard, parental love is even more ethically circumscribed than either friendship or romantic love, for it is directed toward a very specific and obvious end—the well-being of the child—and insofar as it fails to promote this then it must be accounted a failure. Even the most intense parental affection cannot be justified or redeemed if it fails to achieve this end. If we love our children we will naturally want to do what is best for them. We will want them to succeed as separate individuals and not to remain physically or emotionally constrained by the love that should promote their autonomy. And in willing this as an end we must also will the means whereby this can be achieved.

In what follows, I focus on three different aspects of parental love. First, I consider the goal of parental love. Parental love is clearly focused on the well-being of the child, and for the most part, all of the caring and nurturing that parental love involves has the future separation and flourishing of that child as its implicit end. It could only be a deficient form of parental love that promoted dependency or the inability to relate to anyone except one's parents. In this section, I use three literary depictions of parent-child relations, from Dickens, Balzac, and Toni Morrison, to illuminate the proper perspective and the dialectic that subtends parental love. I argue against the idea that parental love is basically a matter of training or control, since love requires a much deeper involvement than the idea of "training" implies.

In the next section, I consider parental love as it is typically embodied in the everyday activities and relations between parents and children today, and I ask about the significance of this kind of love. Given that most child caring is repetitious and routine, it would seem particularly difficult to exalt parental love to the same level as friendship or romance. How can a love be deep and profoundly satisfying when it is tied so completely to the minutiae of everyday life? In what sense is it "meaningful," and in what sense is it significant for the individuals involved?

Finally, I look toward the future. With the emergence of new reproductive technologies and the future possibilities of cloning, eugenics, and test-tube babies, it may seem that we are approaching a time when parental love will be less relevant, less necessary, and considered more of a historical episode than a part of the natural order of things. Perhaps our future society will come to resemble the ideal Republic that Plato described, in which actual paternity and maternity is irrelevant in the greater community of all. The full advent of this new technology may still be a long way off. But even at this point, the very possibility of something that had previously been inconceivable forces us to think about alternative families and forms of parenting. Is it in the interests of our children to repudiate the traditional family unit that is rightfully associated with so much psychological damage and abuse? Or would the ideal collective community, Platonic or otherwise, be one that is actually lacking in love? At the end of this chapter I address such issues in order to evaluate the future of parental love.

The Goal of Parental Love

Every kind of relationship has its own natural trajectory, an arc that describes the course of its typical fulfillment or decline. All things being equal, for example, a friendship between two good people should endure because both of the friends are committed to moral goodness, and so their relationship is mutually enhancing. But a friendship between someone who is good and someone who is not will eventually come to grief because the friends do not have the same priority. In one traditional model of romantic love, the lovers are fired by separation and withdrawal, but their passion declines once the mystery of the other person becomes all too familiar and known. However, a different account of postromantic love promises more sustained possibilities of personal fulfillment.

In the case of parental love, the natural trajectory of the relationship is easier to discern. At the outset, children are completely dependent on their parents, who literally have the power of life and death over them. But as the children grow up they will become less dependent. Through the nurturing of their parents they should grow physically, spiritually, and emotionally until they are in a relevant sense "self-sufficient" and ready to live by themselves, although this need not always involve physical separation. At such a point it may be emotionally difficult for most parents to let their children go, but at a deeper level they "know" that this is the right thing, since the whole of their parenting has been geared toward their children's autonomy and personal fulfillment. Indeed, their work as parents would be incomplete if their children continued to believe that they could not function without them. Thus, the relationship between parents and children is initially one-sided, since all the caring and nurturing must be on the part of the parents. As the child matures, however, the relationship will become more reciprocal, as the parents take account of the child's own personality and needs and allow themselves to be affected by them. And finally, this circle of caring may complete itself when parents are older and need the help of their children in order to function and survive.

In this respect, then, the natural goal of the parent-child relationship is the child's own separation and well-being. More than the periodic outburst of affection, to love one's child must involve giving sustained attention to whatever will achieve this end, since this is what is good for the child. Thus in some situations a parent should establish rules both for the child's own safety and so the child can develop good relations with others. Hitting another child must be punished, and going to school is usually required, even if the child does not feel like it. For even though it may avoid aggravation, not to offer any real guidance and just to let the child be does not help the child in the long run. He or she will not have a strong sense of what is important and will find it hard to get along with others. On the other hand, a totally controlling parent is one who ignores the individual nature of his or her own child. If a child has no musical talents, then probably that child should not be made to practice music endlessly; if a child is naturally shy, then there is something wrong with forcing that child to participate on a team. As these examples show, there is a dialectic of responsiveness and control that subtends parental love, and to love one's child is to be aware at some level of this process and to be reflectively concerned about it. Should I make him pay for the window that he broke? Is she old enough to walk home by herself? Did I let myself become too angry? All of these questions and many more that arise in the context of the parent's love for his or her child testify to an absolute concern, which is often expressed as guilt, for the emotional, spiritual, and physical well-being of the child and for the ultimate goal of the child's autonomy. They are not simply moral questions that concern what is right and wrong at any particular point, for they arise in the context of a projected goal and an end, which is the child's own maturity. In this respect, sometimes we should enforce the rule to affirm a principle that we think is important, while sometimes it may be more appropriate to forget the rule if we think that the child needs to know that he or she is more important than it.

Thus the parent's love for his or her child, which often seems the most automatic and intuitive kind of love, is actually the most "thoughtful" kind of love and requires a continual reflection on the parent-child relationship itself. As we have seen, the sheer proliferation of contemporary literature on childcare makes things even more complicated for parents, making our dealings with our children more fraught with anxiety than they ever have been before. But at the same time, not to be reflective and concerned about these things, to rely unthinkingly on a system of child rearing or to allow the child to do whatever he or she wants, is really to be unconcerned about the child and his or her well-being and opposed to the tendency of love.

So far, then, I have argued that there is a dialectic of control and letting be that underlies the parent-child relation, and that the goal of this dialectic is the autonomy and well-being of the child. The goal of both friendship and romantic love is, largely, the perpetuation of the relationship itself, in the sense that people do not usually become friends or lovers because they have an ulterior motive that goes beyond their desire for relation. But in the case of parental love, the welfare and flourishing of the child is the most important thing, and as parents we can even anticipate a time when our children may no longer view the relationship with their parents as one that is especially important to them. Indeed, parents will sometimes sacrifice themselves and even their own relationship to their children in order to achieve this end—for example, not living with one's child because one realizes that this may be best for her, or giving up one's claim of parenthood if this would be the only way of preserving that child's life. In the Bible story in which two women come to King Solomon each claiming to be the mother of the same child, it is the real mother who abandons her claim rather than allowing her child to be cut in half. Such a sacrifice is possible, I think, because we recognize that the child's dependency on its parent is only temporary and not the most fundamental aspect of who that child is. By contrast, its self-sufficiency and well-being is something that cannot even be provisionally rejected in the name of parental love.

We can now reflect more closely on the goal of parental love by looking at three literary examples that should help to make things clearer. First, the overbearing and controlling parent Mr. Gradgrind in Dickens's *Hard Times*, whose inflexible system of child rearing is emotionally and spiritually disastrous for his children. Next, the doting parent in Balzac's novel *Pere Goriot*, who lives so completely for his children that he fails to offer them any real guidance in life. And finally, the more ambivalent case of Sethe, the mother in Toni Morrison's *Beloved* who kills her own child rather than have her captured and brought up under slavery. Reflection on these three cases can help us become clearer about parental love in the best sense and the nature of its goal.

Hard Times is ostensibly a novel about the evils of industrialism and commercial life. The story takes place in the drab polluted city of Cokeville, where all human aspirations and feelings are sacrificed to the need for profit. Mr. Gradgrind is a retired industrialist who embodies the new capitalist spirit, even in his relationship to his own children, Louisa and Tom:

> Thomas Gradgrind, sir. A man of realities. A man of facts and calculations. A man who proceeds upon the principle that two and two are four, and nothing over, and who is not to be talked into allowing for anything over. Thomas Gradgrind, sir—peremptorily Thomas—Thomas Gradgrind. With a rule and a pair of scales, and the multiplication table always in his pocket, sir, ready to weigh and measure any parcel of human nature, and tell you exactly what it comes to. It is a mere question of figures, a case of simple arithmetic.[9]

Mr. Gradgrind cannot see the point of human sentiment such as love or affectionate caring or of anything that has to do with the imagination. He scorns play and every activity that is not ultimately "productive" in the narrow capitalist sense and anchored in the reality of facts. He has founded a model school with Mr. Bounderby and brought up his own children along the lines of this system:

> No little Gradgrind had ever seen a face in the moon; it was up in the moon before it could speak distinctly. No little Gradgrind had ever learnt the silly jingle, Twinkle, twinkle, little star; how I wonder what you are! No little Gradgrind had ever known wonder on the subject, each little Gradgrind having at five years old dissected the Great Bear like a professor Owen, and driven Charles's Wain like a locomotive engine-driver. No little Gradgrind had ever associated a cow in a field with that famous cow with the crumpled horn who tossed the dog who worried the cat who killed the rat who ate the malt or with that yet more famous cow who swallowed Tom Thumb: it had never heard of those celebrities, and had only been introduced to a cow as a graminivorous ruminating quadruped with several stomachs.[10]

Because the children's mother, Mrs. Gradgrind, is ineffectual and apparently half-crazy, Mr. Gradgrind has had full rein to impose his theories on his children, and in *Hard Times* the results are shown to be disastrous. When Gradgrind approaches his daughter with a marriage proposal from the local industrialist Mr. Bounderby, he begins as follows:

> "My dear Louisa, . . . You have been so well trained, and you do, I am happy to say, so much justice to the education you have received, that I have perfect confidence in your good sense. You are not impulsive, you are not romantic, you are accustomed to view everything from the strong dispassionate ground of reason and calculation. From that ground alone, I know you will view and consider what I am going to communicate."[11]

Having been taught to suppress every sentimental and romantic notion as irrelevant, Louisa has no emotional response. She just comments impassively, "What does it matter?" She replies to her father: "The baby-preference that even I have heard of as common among children, has never had its innocent resting-place in my breast. You have been so careful of me that I never had a child's heart. You have trained me so well that I never dreamed a child's dream. You have dealt so wisely with me, Father, from my cradle to this hour, that I never had a child's belief or a child's fear."[12] Only later, after living with Bounderby, who is thirty years her senior and another version of her father's ideal, does she become more explicitly aware of all that her father's system has destroyed in her own soul. And so she turns on her father and condemns him:

> "How could you give me life, and take from me all the inappreciable things that raise it from the state of conscious death? Where are the graces of my soul? Where are the sentiments of my heart? What have you done, oh, Father, what have you done, with the garden that should have bloomed once, in this great wilderness here. . . . I don't reproach you, Father. What you have never nurtured in me, you have never nurtured in yourself; but oh! if you had only done so, long ago, or if you had only neglected me, what a much better and happier creature I should have been this day!"[13]

In the end, we are told, Louisa is condemned to a loveless life made all the more painful by her final recognition of what it is that she has never had. Likewise, her brother Tom, who is cheerless and mean throughout, responds to the misery of his upbringing by robbing the bank and planting the blame for it on another. He has been taught the virtue of personal advancement, and he has no sympathy for the feelings or the rights of others. By the end of the novel, Gradgrind finally realizes the impoverishment of his own point of view.

Clearly, Gradgrind's system is totally inappropriate and mistaken, for it leads to disastrous results. By emphasizing facts and the irrelevance of sentiment and everything belonging to the imagination, Gradgrind's system produces children who are miserable because they are so emotionally misshapen. It could be argued that Gradgrind is only a caricature, and that the whole of *Hard Times* is an unfair attack on Jeremy Bentham, John Stuart Mill, and their utilitarian philosophy. The irony is that Mill's own father used something like Gradgrind's system to educate his son. The young John Stuart Mill is famous for being able to read Greek at the age of three. But if we needed an actual illustration of the impoverishment of this approach, we have only to consider Mill's mental collapse and his complete emotional breakdown at the age of nineteen.[14] But the main point is that Gradgrind imposes his ideas on his children without any attempt to relate to the latter as individual beings who have their own specific qualities, desires, and needs. He never appreciates or cherishes the special nature of each of his children, but instead imposes an educational agenda upon them that is largely reflective of his own values and ideals. In a sense he tries to recreate himself through his own children. And however energetic and supposedly well meaning he claims to be, his love is narcissism; it is purely self-regarding and indifferent to the specificity of his children, who need something more than this in order to flourish and thrive.

To love someone, we might say, involves cherishing someone and recognizing that person as another subject in the world, and hence not treating him or her as an object that needs to be produced or improved. It also involves being very much aware of the beloved's desires and needs; on occasion, this may require us to suspend our own views of what is important and the way that things should be. Parental love in particular is about trying to see the beloved accurately and to understand what he or she is all about. We should not be on the lookout for signs of ourselves in our children, for this constitutes a rejection of their own specific nature, which often resists whatever plans or goals we might have for them.

Interestingly enough, *Hard Times* describes another relationship between a parent and a child that is defective for exactly the opposite reasons. Mr. Bounderby, the local factory owner who becomes Louisa's husband, prides himself on his independent, self-made status. He tells everyone who will listen that his mother abandoned him, and how, thrust out by his grandparents, he was forced to fend for himself; eventually, though, by sheer strength of will he made himself the wealthiest citizen in Coketown. The reality, however, is that Bounderby's parents were decent shopkeepers. But for the sake of appearances and her son's self-serving myth, his mother, Mrs. Pegler, has agreed never to visit him or even to talk about him without his permission. She is a doting parent who cannot refuse her son anything. And since she is a doting parent, she travels into Coketown every year just to look at her son and to revel in his achievement. As a parent, Mrs. Pegler is the opposite of Gradgrind because she has no expectations of her child, and instead of offering him direction in life, she takes her direction from him, with the result that Bounderby is an unpleasant, uncharitable, mean-spirited boor.

In Balzac's *Pere Goriot*, we are shown another parent who lives only for his children. Goriot cannot refuse his daughters anything, and so he is largely responsible for their own misery and inability to cope. Balzac writes:

> The upbringing he gave his daughters was of course preposterous. Goriot's income was over sixty thousand francs, and he spent no more than twelve hundred a year on himself. His sole joy lay in gratifying the caprices of his daughters. The very best instructors were engaged to teach them the accomplishments that are considered part of a good education. . . . They went riding, they had a carriage, they lived as the mistresses of a wealthy old lord might have lived; they had only to express even the most extravagant wish, and their father would rush to execute it; he demanded no more than a caress in return. Goriot put his daughters on a level with the angels, and naturally, poor man! far above himself. He even loved their acts of unkindness.[15]

Later, as his own misery grows, he exclaims, "When we lived in the Rue de la Jussienne, they didn't have to use their brains, they knew nothing about the world; they just loved me. Oh God, why didn't they stay young forever. . . ?"[16] When his daughters marry he settles practically the whole of his fortune on them. But the more he gives, the more he is spurned. At first, he lives with each of his daughters, but he becomes a real embarrassment to them. He moves into lodgings, and the small annuity he has kept for himself is gradually eaten away by the need to pay for his daughters' extravagances and the gambling debts of their lovers.

In this way he goes on, totally devoted and even idolizing his daughters to such a point that he really has no life beyond theirs: "Whenever it's a fine day," he explains,

> "I find out from their maids if my daughters are going out, and I go to the Champs-Elysees and wait for them to pass. My heart leaps up when I see their carriages coming. I admire the way they're dressed, they throw me a little smile as they go past, and it lights up the whole day for me like a burst of sunshine. . . . Aren't they my own flesh and blood? I love the horses that draw them, I wish I were a little dog on their laps. I live in their pleasures. We all have different ways of loving: mine does no one any harm, so why should anyone bother about me?"[17]

Goriot feels that as a father, his one obligation is to keep giving to his daughters. As he explains: "Fathers have to be always giving, if they're to be happy. Always giving: that's what being a father means."[18] He gives up all of his possessions. Even more, he gives up his own life. At the end when he has nothing left, his anguish is because he can no longer give to them. As he is dying, one daughter is at a dance and the other is at the theater.

Goriot seems to love his daughters with an inexhaustible devotion, which impresses Rastignac, the young hero of the novel, because he has already realized the fickleness and inconstancy of all romantic affection by comparison. But in what sense is Goriot's devotion really love? I think it would probably be more appropriate to see it as a form of self-abandonment and the desire to live through another rather than to live for oneself. We are told, for example, that Goriot's great love began when his wife died, which makes it seem likely that his devotion to his daughters was driven by his desire to escape his own anguish and grief. It is a psychological subterfuge that allows him to avoid his unhappiness by living as a supplement to his own children's lives. But whatever explanation may be most appropriate here, the fact is his daughters are basically unhappy, in spite of their wealth and noble marriages. Their father never gave them any real guidance; he only responded to their desires and needs. And so his affection, while it is great, cannot really be regarded as the deepest or most authentic form of parental love. Like the good parent, Goriot is able to empty himself and forget about his own problems for the sake of his children, but he does not do this so he can then step back into himself in order to help them. In fact, he seems to idolize them in order to avoid himself. Here there is self-abandonment, but no self-giving.

In effect, Dickens and Balzac offer us two different extremes in parental love: one that imposes a system or a set of principles on the child that effectively destroys the child's own individual nature, and one that measures love in terms of self-sacrifice and self-abandonment for the child's immediate needs, but which leaves the child unguided and unprepared for life. If, as I have argued, to love one's child involves doing whatever is best for that child and helping him or her to achieve self-sufficiency and well-being, then these are both deficient forms of parental love. Interestingly enough, they both fail for the same reason: In the end they embody strategies of loving that refuse a real involvement with the child. The first treats the child as a pure object, to be shaped and manipulated; the second treats the child as a pure subject, when this is really the goal and the achievement of parental love and certainly not a basic given.

I suggested earlier that the real dialectic of parental love is one of control and allowing to be. Parents are to a great extent in charge of this process, and they must choose when it is appropriate to insist on a principle and when it would be more appropriate to reconsider for the sake of the child. This implies that parents must also be moved and affected by their children and discover depths and issues within themselves at the same time as they seek to nurture their children. Perhaps like all other loves—although we do not always recognize this—the authentic form of parental love is reciprocal or dialogical in character. It must involve the continual possibility of self-transformation in the shared space where lover and beloved exist. If I simply bring up my children in the right way but remain unaffected by them, then it must follow that I am basically uninvolved with them, and all my love is more like caretaking than authentic caring.

In Toni Morrison's *Beloved* we have a final literary work against which to test our intuitions concerning parental love. *Beloved* is set in the South and in Ohio in the years immediately before and after the Civil War. In the novel, Sethe is a slave woman who suffers unspeakably at the hands of her slave masters. Eventually she escapes with her children to the North, but a few days after she arrives her owners find her and try to return her to the plantation. Sethe is trapped, but in desperation she decides that she cannot return to slavery and so she decides to kill her own children: "I couldn't let all that go back to where it was," she explains, "and I couldn't let her nor any of em live under schoolteacher. That was out."[19] She manages to kill her infant daughter, Beloved, before she is prevented from killing the others. Now there is no doubt that Sethe is a good and caring mother. On her flight North, for example, she is absolutely driven by the need to be connected to her baby, and she is able to articulate the necessity of this bond with some real power:

> All I knew was I had to get my milk to my baby girl. Nobody was going to nurse her like me. Nobody was going to get it to her fast enough, or take it away when she had enough and didn't know it. Nobody knew that she couldn't pass her air if you held her up on your shoulder, only if she was lying on my knees. Nobody knew that but me and nobody had her milk but me.[20]

She has never known a mother's love herself, because her own mother was hanged when she was young, but this only makes her more aware of how important a mother's care is:

> I wouldn't draw breath without my children. I told Baby Suggs that and she got down on her knees to beg God's pardon for me. Still, it's so. My plan was to take us all to the other side where my own ma'am is. They stopped me from getting us there, but they didn't stop you from getting here. Ha ha. You came right on back like a good girl, like a daughter which is what I wanted to be and would have been if my ma'am had been able to get out of the rice long enough before they hanged her and let me be one. You know what? She'd had the bit so many times she smiled. When she wasn't smiling she smiled, and I never saw her own smile. I wonder what they was doing when they was caught. Running, you think? No. Not that. Because she was my ma'am and nobody's ma'am would run off and leave her daughter, would she?[21]

Sethe is condemned by the whole black community for killing Beloved, especially since in later years she does not seem remorseful or regretful for what she has done. Perhaps we might say that even if her action is wrong it is at least understandable because of the extreme circumstances. The institution of slavery corrupts all human relationships, for under slavery everything becomes a matter of personal property and possession, and even maternity is reduced to a matter of ownership that someone has the right to dispose of at will. But even though her action is shocking, there is, I think, a sense in which it can be justified as the expression of a mother's love in such a circumstance. Sethe knew the physical and psychological ravages of slavery, and she understood that if she returned to the plantation her children would be made to suffer in the same way that she had, and probably, as in her own case, without a mother who could protect them. Hence the proper goal of her love, the well-being and self-sufficiency of her child—could never be achieved, and under these circumstances she kills Beloved. It is important to realize, then, that her action is not self-interested or self-regarding. She is not thinking in terms of some greater good, or responding, like Abraham, to a higher commandment that has been placed on her. She kills her child, but from the perspective of a mother's love this is her own act of sacrifice, because she could not bear to let them do to her own children what they had already done to herself. It is an act of mercy that is not done in order to relieve the mother's distress. In fact, it makes it far worse. Whether right or wrong, it is done for the ultimate well-being of Beloved.

Other slave narratives and cases of the time suggest that Sethe's response was by no means unique. Under slavery, many women simply refused to have children, while others killed their children, not out of selfishness or as a matter of principle in opposition to the slave system, but as a desperate and final act of love and caring. Certainly, the example from *Beloved* is morally ambivalent, and there is some real question about what Sethe's motivations were, but at the same time it helps to clarify the final goal of parental love, and the despair that is provoked when it cannot be achieved.

In the *Nicomachean Ethics*, Aristotle argues that there are some inevitable limits to friendship and the love of one's friend. He argues, for example, that no one would ever want a friend to become a god, for even though this would be the greatest good for one's friend, it would imply the end of the friendship since the gods do not need us and there can be no personal relations between humans and gods. Similarly, in romantic love the lovers often torture themselves and make each other miserable for the sake of the relationship that they are unwilling to give up. In *The Sorrows of Young Werther*, Werther forces his attentions on Lotte even though he realizes that this is detrimental to her own life and happiness. Parental love is different, I think, because the goal of parental love—the autonomy, maturity, and well-being of the child—is often taken to be more important than the maintenance of the relationship itself. And anyone who denies this, or who says that a child should sacrifice everything for his parents, would probably be considered a bad parent whose love is selfishly motivated and not in

the child's best interests. Thus we can forgive, or at least understand, the lover or the friend who secretly welcomes the beloved's
disappointment if this entails the continuation of their relationship.
But since parental love is directed toward the final separation of the
child, and her flourishing as an independent being, we would probably regard such an attitude on the part of the parents as a sign of
their failure and inability to love their child in the deepest possible
way. All of this serves to emphasize the moral aspects of parental
love, which are really primary, and helps us to distinguish between
its good and corrupted forms. In the next section we focus more
closely on this theme by showing how parental love is related to the
moral growth of the parents as well as the children themselves.

Parental Love and Everyday Life

Parental love is the least exalted of all the different kinds of love.
Romantic lovers are supposed to grasp eternity in their mutual
bliss, and true friendship is considered noble and sublime. But by
its very nature, parental love belongs to the everyday realm of rep-
etition and routine, and it involves an almost endless series of
tasks that ensure the well-being of one's child. Of course, there are
times when a child is finally calm and a parent can stand back to
regard the child with an absolute astonishment and wonder: This
is a new life that I have taken responsibility for, an absolute other
who commands me to protect and provide. But these moments are
only temporary. Parental love is usually bound to the minutiae of
everyday life and to the relentless necessity of making meals,
washing clothes, nursing and preventing sickness, keeping things
clean, and keeping things calm. Therefore it is difficult to gauge
the philosophical significance of parental love, since it does not
measure itself in terms of an absolute or yearn for some ultimate
point of transcendence. It is ongoing, repetitive, and routine. And
for parents, it is usually enough, and even fulfilling, if this state
continues without any upset or end. Sometimes it is assumed that
the truly philosophical standpoint must involve an escape from
the cave of everydayness and a turning away from our usual
absorption in the mundane details of life. But when we love a child
and take care of her, most of our concerns, thoughts, and activities
are fixed on this routine level. We cannot really escape from this
level if we love our children and want to take care of them properly. How then are we to understand the philosophical significance
of parental love—its ultimate meaning and value—if by its very
nature it resists every sublimation or movement of transcendence?

And given its demanding nature, how can such a relationship be truly satisfying and contribute to our own sense of personal fulfillment?

Another problem presents itself from the outset: Historically, mothers have usually been the primary caregivers of children, while fathers have often been absent and encouraged to seek their fulfillment outside the home. It may be argued that this has intensified the emotional disfigurement of men and their comparative lack of nurturing skills, and without doubt it has largely confined women to the domestic economy of the household and reduced the whole of their nature to the single activity of motherhood. As Adrienne Rich comments in her own memoir of motherhood, *Of Woman Born*: "For most of what we know as the 'mainstream' of recorded history, Motherhood as an institution has ghettoized and degraded female potentialities."[22] Given such a context, it is not surprising that parental love, and a mother's love in particular, may sometimes be viewed as a burdensome duty and that one's children may then become the most tangible expression of one's own reduction and loss. And yet, most parents understand at some level that their children are not responsible for confining them. Even in the most extreme cases, such as when a mother is left with several children to care for by herself, a woman may see her maternal work as the most fulfilling and important aspect of who she is. As Shulamith Firestone explains, the institution of motherhood that has often been used to suppress and remove female possibilities must be distinguished from the authentic possibilities of maternal love: "The mother who wants to kill her child for what she has had to sacrifice for it learns to love the same child only when she understands it is also helpless and oppressed as she is by her oppressor. Then hatred is directed outwards and motherlove is born."[23]

The activities associated with parenting may be mundane, relentless, and exhausting, but when a child is obviously flourishing and happy the parent can experience a most profound sense of joy and well-being. And to be given a sign that our love is recognized and returned—in a baby's smile, for example is an indication that our love has begun to achieve its projected goal. An active involvement in the flourishing of another being is probably one of the most ecstatic and rewarding experiences that one could possibly have. This suggests that the "labor" of parental love actually involves a very profound and sustained attunement to the real order of life, in the sense of being guided by that which is most fundamental and important. From this perspective the philosophical significance of parental love becomes much clearer. It is a sustained work of nurturance and creation and a more or less complete giving of oneself to another who needs protection and caring. This love seeks the well-being of the other person more than anything else. But in opposition to the traditional image of parenthood, and motherhood in particular, such a complete generosity does not have to involve self-abandonment or loss. Indeed, when we are able to care devotedly for someone else, such as a child, we can also experience an intrinsic sense of connection, a corresponding enlargement of being, and a real sense of attunement to the movement of life itself.

What is most undeniable is the intensity of the love that parents can have for their children. It may not always be expressed in obviously "loving" ways—indeed, annoyance and anger may often prevail—but lying beneath the vicissitudes of the moment there is usually an underlying involvement and concern and a complete identification with the joys and sorrows of that child. We are proud and happy when that child is successful, but we feel that child's pain and disappointment just as keenly as if her pain were our own, if not more so. Most parents would probably do anything for their children and would not hesitate for a moment if asked to sacrifice for them. This much seems intuitively obvious and unremarkable. But we must ask, what is the origin and the basis of such overwhelming love? And how can this sacrifice ultimately be experienced as enhancing and rewarding for the parents themselves? It may or may not be a biological given that compels us to love our offspring in this way, and it may be that different versions of parental love have been promoted and valorized in our history. Sometimes, as we have seen, parental love has not been as powerful as other factors. But can we now say something about the essential significance of this love and how it can appeal so strongly to us?

In the *Symposium*, Plato argues that the desire to have children is really an expression of our ordinary desire for immortality. The philosopher, the poet, and the statesman may produce great books or great deeds that will live in popular memory long after they have died, but for most people, Plato claims, the only kind of personal immortality that they can achieve is through their own children and the continuation of a line of descent. "This is how every mortal creature perpetuates itself," Diotima tells Socrates.

> It cannot, like the divine, be still the same throughout eternity; it can only leave behind new life to fill the vacancy that is left in its species

by obsolescence. This, my dear Socrates, is how the body and all else that is temporal partakes of the eternal; there is no other way. And so every creature prizes its own issue, since the whole creation is inspired by this love, this passion for immortality.[24]

This reasoning, however, is oblivious to the child's own specific nature and treats that child as a means to an end that is ultimately selfish.

Similarly, when Freud discusses the way in which parents are usually devoted to their children, he explicitly uses the term *narcissism* to emphasize that this is a relationship that is ultimately self-regarding. As he comments:

> If we look at the attitude of affectionate parents towards their children, we have to recognize that it is a revival and reproduction of their own narcissism which they have long since abandoned. The trustworthy pointer constituted by overvaluation, which we have already recognized as a narcissistic stigma in the case of object-choice, dominates, as we all know, their emotional attitude. Thus they are under a compulsion to ascribe every perfection to the child—which sober observation would find no occasion to do—and to conceal and forget all his shortcomings.[25]

Freud argues that the parent's love for his or her children is founded on self-deception, for like Plato, Freud believes that we live through our children and come to terms with our own mortality by projecting our deepest hopes and desires onto their lives. We come to accept that we cannot live for ever, but that our children will survive. Hence, Freud continues:

> The child shall fulfil those wishful dreams of the parents which they never carried out—the boy shall become a great man and a hero in his father's place, and the girl shall marry a prince as a tardy compensation for her mother. At the most touchy point in the narcissistic system, the immortality of the ego, which is so hard pressed by reality, security is achieved by taking refuge in the child. Parental love, which is so moving and at bottom so childish, is nothing but the parents' narcissism born again, which, transformed into object-love, unmistakably reveals its former nature.[26]

There is probably a lot of truth in the Platonic or Freudian position. Many people are very deeply concerned about having and raising their *own* children. They might regard adoption as an acceptable option, but they think of it as second best. The question of actual paternity is still a determinant of love. Likewise, there is a sense in which the child's growth and development allows us to relive and transcend our own childhood at a mediated remove. Maybe we want our children to be like us and to have the same interests and passions as we did. While we would respect a friend's desire to pursue an interest or a goal that is not one that we would share, it is not unlikely that we would try to change our children's goals or desires so that they conform more closely to our own. It is hard for some parents to accept that their children do not want to continue the family business or have the same religious beliefs as their parents. In this respect, it is undeniable that parental love has a narcissistic and self-regarding quality. In its most extreme form this is expressed in the appropriative relationship that regards the child as *mine* or as my property that I can order and dispose of just as I will.

The problem, though, is that only a debased or deficient form of love insists on its own power and priority, for it thereby reduces the other, the so-called beloved, to the status of an object to be processed and ordered in the subject's own terms. Love in its most authentic sense involves an intense appreciation of the other person, and this means that we must cherish the beloved and allow her to be herself. In the case of children, this involves helping them to discover their own weaknesses and strengths, their own talents, and their own moral good. It does not entail being totally permissive and letting our children find themselves by doing whatever they want. But it does mean that when we impose rules and structure on their lives, it is so that they can more easily determine themselves. When I look at my child I should not be trying to discover myself at an earlier point in my own life. This is an easy temptation, and it may help me to understand what my child might be living through at this point. But a deeper love would recognize the presence of another person, someone who is absolutely different from me who has her own needs and requirements. As Sara Ruddick puts it:

> The ordinary secular mother [or father] also learns to ask "What are you going through?" and to wait to hear the answer rather than giving it. She learns to ask again and keep listening even if she cannot make sense of what she hears or can barely tolerate the child she has understood. Attention is akin to the capacity for empathy, the ability to suffer or celebrate with another as if in the other's experience you know and find yourself. However, the idea of empathy, as it is pop-

ularly understood, underestimates the importance of knowing another *without* finding yourself in her. A mother really looks at her child, tries to see him accurately rather than herself in him.[27]

In pregnancy, the same intuition and astonishment is often evoked by the being inside oneself—that here is another person who is both a part of oneself and yet absolutely different, who must be protected and cared for. This experience of the essential mystery of the other person is an essential part of all love, including parents' love for their children. With a sense of wonder the mother experiences the development of the child inside her until that child is born, separate and with an identity of its own. But as the child grows, the parents will continue to be astonished by this being who can never be their property or possession. In fact, all of their work is to promote the child's autonomy and connection to others and to prepare for that time when he or she will no longer be dependent on them.

Thus, while there are certainly aspects of narcissism in parental love, whereby through a process of identification we incorporate the child's life as a part of our own and share her joys and sorrows, it is the caring and concern for one who is absolutely different that prevails at the deeper level. This is, of course, a moral task, and in a sense it is the most fundamental moral task there is—to guide another being into the region of goodness and to foster the development of that individual, to help him become both self-sustaining and connected with others. To love a child, in fact, and thereby to teach that child how to love others. Parental love involves moral work of a complex nature. Loving one's child means that one is prepared to do whatever must be done to nurture that child, to protect her, to educate her, and to make her into a decent human being. Going beyond this however, to love one's child also involves an idealization of that child's nature. I do not mean an *idolization* of the child, such as Freud described, for this involves an inherent self-deception and a blindness that will ultimately be injurious to the child herself. In an idealizing projection, we seize on all that is good in the child and allow her to grasp the possibility of her own moral goodness. We must remain realistic about what the child is capable of, but at the same time we offer the child a vision of herself as morally good that the child is capable of pursuing. As Nel Noddings puts it so eloquently: "When we attribute the best possible motive consonant with reality to the cared-for, we confirm him; that is, we reveal to him an attainable image of himself that is lovelier than that manifested in his present acts. In an important sense, we embrace him as one with us in devotion to caring."[28] Thus, parental love is like friendship and romantic love at its best because it gives the beloved an enticing vision of her ideal self that she may then seek to aspire to.

It is important to note, however, that the moral activity that is expressed in parental love cannot be reduced to a simple set of parental duties without distorting or reducing the nature of that love. From something like a Kantian perspective, it might be possible to specify the duties that one owes to one's children—to preserve them from danger, to make sure they are properly nourished and provided for, to teach them how to get on in the world, to teach them the difference between right and wrong, and to make sure that they can deal with the needs of other people. Through such training, the child may become competent and self-sufficient, which is one of the most important goals of parental love. But such guidance remains training and not love if the parent remains completely unmoved and unchanged by all of his or her dealings with the child. As we have seen, love must always imply the possibility of a mutual transformation and growth, for this is what being open to another and taking him seriously means: that I am moved and affected by what is moving and affecting to him, and I am prepared to change my own desires, or put them on hold, because I grasp his desires as equally important. But if I am intent on doing my duty and remain fixed and unmoved by the child, then I am really closed off from him and I will never undergo the risk of personal transformation that love requires. On the other hand, if I decide to devote myself at every moment and in every possible way to my children, then I will also be unable to experience this ongoing transformation, for I have already abandoned that self which should be transformed in its dealings with my children.

Thus our love and caring for our children is inherently moral, not only in terms of the beloved but also in terms of our own development and progress: In bringing up a child we are constantly challenged, frustrated, and overwhelmed. And in dealing with each new crisis and situation that presents itself, we are forced to question our own priorities and ways of thinking. In this respect there is a strong connection between parental love and moral growth. If all our caring consisted in the imposition of fixed principles, we could never really respond to the other and never really be transformed by her. But in caring for my child I accomplish a moral work that brings me closer to goodness. It makes me a better person by cultivating patience and humility and the ability to respond to others. The object of this moral activity, the child, is ultimately the expression of my own moral ideal: In a sense he or she is my better self, and so I am ready to sacrifice everything for the child if this should be required.

So far, then, two levels of significance have been described that help us understand the significance of parental love. First, there *is* a sense in which it is a narcissistic and self-regarding form of love. Our children are extensions of ourselves, and they allow us to reexperience our own childhood at a mediated remove. But parental love is also at its best an inherently moral activity whose goal is the moral and physical well-being of the beloved, which involves the moral enhancement and growth of the parent as well. Finally, and in addition to these two other levels, it can be argued that to care for someone in an everyday and ongoing way, as we care for our children, is itself a pure act of generosity and gratitude to life itself. If we are not overwhelmed by our situation, we will experience our caring and love not as a moral obligation that is imposed on us but as a joyful devotion, not just to another person but, in a sense, to the movement of life itself. We do not really need recognition or thanks for what we are doing. Of course, such things are helpful and encourage us to maintain our attitude as ones who care. But we also know that we will continue to love our children even if they make huge mistakes or move away and create lives for themselves that only include us in a marginal way. We recognize that at some point our children will grow up. This is the way it should be, and then they will not particularly need us. We hope that they will continue to love us. But what we hope for most of all—and this is the best sign that our love has been successful—is that our children will be able to love and care for others as we have loved them. Perhaps they will have their own children and will continue the circle of caring. All of this is an act of gratitude to life and shows our deepest attunement to it.

At those times when we *are* overwhelmed by all that caring for our children entails, we will long for an escape. Given the relentless succession of dinners, appointments, clothes to wash, and rooms to clean, we may become deeply alienated from the domestic realm that parental love ordains. If there is no other outlet, nothing apart from the routine domestic round that would allow us to put things in context, then we may become dispirited or angry with our children or angry at ourselves for being angry since this is not what parental love is supposed to involve. But given a space in which parental love can be fostered, then the everyday routines that are involved in caring for our children, the whole minutiae of ordinary life, will become something that we will be able to appreciate and enjoy. Once again, Noddings puts this very well:

> The one-caring, then, is not bored with ordinary life. As the Christian-Catholic finds new truth and strength in repeated celebrations of the mass, so the one-caring finds new delight in breakfast, in welcoming home her wanderers, in feeding the cat who purrs against her ankle, in noticing the twilight. She does not ask, "Is this all there is?," but wishes in hearty affirmation that what-is might go on and on.[29]

Thus, the significance of the everyday, or what Nietzsche called the "depth" of the present moment, is revealed through the ongoing joy of parental love. As we continue to care for the child from one moment to the next, we may become aware of our strength in caring and of our complete involvement in the process of life itself.

The Family and Its Future

At this particular point in history, we are very keenly aware of the possibilities of biomedical engineering and the future prospects of cloning, surrogacy, and a pregnancy that may begin and one day continue within the test tube and so avoid the lived relationship to any particular parent. Perhaps humanity is about to enter a new age, which we must either affirm or resist, or perhaps these are only speculative possibilities of science that will fail to materialize. But in either case, the raising of such possibilities, and their prevalence in popular thought, forces us to rethink the natural necessity of parental love, in what respect the traditional forms of parental love are ultimately beneficial and harmful, and whether or not parental love can have a future in a world in which the traditional order of the family—mother, father, child—is increasingly being challenged and undermined.

The relationship between parent and child would seem to be the most important relationship for understanding the development of love, since it is the original source and experience of all our loving. Through the intense and sustained involvement with another person who cares devotedly for us—usually, though not exclusively, the mother—we learn how to love. In being cared for we learn how to care for others. And so we may become autonomous and loving individuals, capable of friendship and romantic love, humanitarian love, and parental love of our own.

But at the same time, it may be said that all of our difficulties in loving derive from the same point. It can be urged that the intensity and exclusivity of the traditional family structure creates future expectations about love that can never be fulfilled. The patriarchal structure of the traditional family distorts all of our future loving and leaves us alienated and bereft. According to one version of Freud, we spend our adult lives trying to recreate the primary and original relationship that we experienced within the original family; this is an impossible goal, however, and one that is often productive of the deepest misery. So what should be our final attitude toward parental love? Should we continue to affirm it uncritically as an absolute good? Or should we now reconsider it in the light of these criticisms of the family as the original locus of alienation, oppression, and control?

Perhaps one way to begin to unravel these questions is to look at two Utopian works of literature that are very different from each other but that both describe the raising of children in a general community. In these communities, none are considered parents in the particular sense of being father or mother to one child but not to another, because all the adults are considered to be "guardians" or "mothers" to all of the children in their charge. Both Plato in *The Republic* and Charlotte Perkins Gilman in *Herland* recognize the danger of particular attachments and the exclusivity of parental love, and so they construct ideal societies in which particularity is overcome through the submersion of all separate identities within the common good.

In Book Five of *The Republic*, for example, Plato describes his ideal community, in which "[t]he children shall be common, and . . . no parent shall know its own offspring nor any child its parent."[30] Plato justifies what he calls "the community of women and children" by explaining that any kind of particular affection or possessiveness naturally takes away from one's sense of belonging to the community in general. "But the individualization of these feelings is a dissolvent," Socrates argues, "when some grieve exceedingly and others rejoice at the same happenings to the city and its inhabitants." And hence, "that city is best ordered in which the greatest number use the expression 'mine' and 'not mine' of the same things in the same way."[31] Rousseau adopts a similar position in *The Social Contract:* Any particular interest is in principle opposed to the general interest of the community as a whole. There will always be a tension between private attachments and our attachment to the common good of all; therefore,

both Plato and Rousseau conclude, we must simply excise particular interests and attachments for the sake of the common good.[32]
Of course, we may respond that such a regime is impossible since
it is not based on human nature as we know it. But the whole
point of *The Republic* is to create a social structure that will be able
to mold and transform human nature so that such a regime is able
to perpetuate itself.

Gilman's feminist utopia, *Herland*, describes a different situation: a peaceful community of women, existing without men, for
whom motherhood, in the sense of nurturing life, is everything.

> And the mother instinct, with us so painfully intense, so thwarted
> by conditions, so concentrated in personal devotion to a few, so bit-
> terly hurt by death, disease, or barrenness, and even by the mere
> growth of the children, leaving the mother alone in her empty
> nest—all this feeling with them flowed out in a strong, wide cur-
> rent, unbroken through the generations, deepening and widening
> through the years, including every child in all the land.[33]

In this society, such a maternity is the highlight and the fulfillment
of every woman's life. In relation to this, the children of the community are all cherished and valued to the highest degree. "'The
children in this country," we are told, "are the one center and focus
of all our thoughts. Every step of our advance is always considered
in its effect on them—on the race. You see, we are *Mothers*,' she
repeated, as if in that she had said it all."[34]

It is important to emphasize that *Herland* is not a reactionary
dystopia in which women are reduced to the status of breeding
machines. In *Herland* there is no great division of labor. Women are
able to develop their own talents and skills, and for them, motherhood is the epitome of all their service to nurturance and growth.
Like Plato, Gilman is very much aware of the problematic character of the traditional family as an institution that works against
community feelings. She assumes that without the distortions and
exclusivity of ordinary parental love, children will learn devotion
and service to others and be able to care for each other in a more
authentic way. But the question is whether this is psychologically
and philosophically realistic. Some have suggested that Plato's
account can only be a joke since it describes a possibility that is so
absurd and remote (along with philosopher kings!), while *Herland*
is premised on the impossible idea of a single-sex community that
has overcome all material scarcity. Granted that there are problems
with the traditional family, should we now abandon every attempt

to reconstruct the family and embrace artificial reproduction and communal parenting, or could there be good reason to reconsider the importance of parental love as it is typically conceived?

The Republic and *Herland* describe societies of mutual solidarity and fellow-feeling where every individual has a strong sense of belonging to the community as a whole. What seems unrealistic, however, is to suppose that someone could be brought to this plateau of universal love and fellow feeling without going through a period of emotional and spiritual intimacy with another human being. In the past, this has been provided by parental love. A sense of community, belonging, and love for others is not some kind of a natural state that growing up within certain families leads us away from, for love of any kind requires intimacy. It involves learning how to relate to someone else. And without an intense involvement with another we could never really learn to love others, let alone develop a universal love for all.

Thus I would argue that some kind of a personal intimacy is essential to the development of love and that if children are raised in common, without a parent-child relationship, it would be much more difficult for them to achieve this. At some point we need someone, such as a parent, who loves us fiercely, who thinks of us as special and important, and who is totally concerned about our well-being. Just to be the recipient of general benevolence and good-heartedness is not enough. And it is through being loved intensely and being cherished as a unique and unrepeatable being that the child will learn to love others later.

Of course, we must set against this the damage that the traditional family often inflicts on the child, and the fact that such "love" may often be destructive and smothering for the child in question. Abuse is always a possibility. But this would be because the particular love was a deficient mode of parental love, and not because parental love is by definition oppressive. In a communal society we might have affectionate feelings for everyone else, but it is unclear that such feelings could ever be anything more than altruistic. A diffuse warm-heartedness is not the same thing as love, since it does not focus on the particularity of the beloved. As we have seen, love requires an attention to the beloved and a reorientation in terms of the beloved's perspective. This means that the beloved must be seen as an "other" and not just as someone who is basically the same as me. It is this strong sense of the otherness of the other, or the mystery of the other, that inspires love and makes it possible. In the Utopian communities that Plato and Gilman describe, however, all significant differences have been removed. Therefore, it would be much harder to focus on the particularity of the other person or, correlatively, to have a strong and distinctive sense of one's self.

Whatever may happen in the future with the development of new reproductive technologies, then, if the ability to love is considered an important value, then the withdrawal of parental love would be a loss because it would be much harder for children to learn how to love. A lesser consideration is that parents and guardians would also lose what is one of the most significant aspects of personal development—namely, the ability to give, to nurture, and to sustain another person, the child, who is to be raised to goodness. Being a loving parent helps to encourage and sustain certain values and modes of relationship to others: for example, empathy and patience, the ability to cherish life that is threatened and vulnerable, and the ability to respond to someone else without insisting on one's own set of needs and priorities. All these qualities enhance and promote public life, and they would advance the loving, cooperative societies that Plato and Gilman espouse.

At the outset, I briefly described the history of childhood and considered the significant point that parental love has also undergone a historical development. Love does not have an essential form, and parental love, like all of the other loves, is subject to economic, cultural, and political vicissitudes. By looking at parental love in its contemporary manifestations, and especially by analyzing its projective goal, I have tried to apprehend its value, its strengths, and its possible weaknesses. Presumably this will help us to determine in what sense parental love may continue and whether this will be a good or a bad thing. The task of parenting is relentless, mundane, repetitive, and often overwhelming. But at the same time, the spiritual and emotional rewards are very great, both in terms of an overall attunement to life and in terms of the possibility of personal development through caring. Without these things life would be considerably less significant and fulfilling.

4

For the Love of Humanity

For the most part, it is easy to love our own friends and family, and since we possess a shared history with them, it is not difficult to grasp that our own well-being must be bound up with theirs. But it is much harder to care for a stranger, and to love that person and take account of his or her needs, when there is nothing that we share beyond the fact of our common humanity. In 1913, Albert Schweitzer abandoned a successful career as a theologian and an organist in order to set up a hospital in Lambarene, an outpost in the Cameroon. He certainly had a religious motivation for going there, for he viewed his own life as subject to the calling of God, but it is important to point out that he went there to heal people, not to convert them, and that for the love of humanity he stayed for the next fifty years until his death.

It is hard to sustain such a love, which involves much more than just devotion to the principles of justice. For some it would be impossible unless one could assume a set of religious parameters to support and justify it. Thus it is questionable whether the love of humanity is ultimately modeled on the love of God or whether it is finally independent of religious motives, as each revolutionary call to "fraternity" would seem to imply. In either case, however, it must be said that humanitarian love is a significant contemporary value. It is embodied in the lives of many modern-day "saints" who have worked and even died for the sake of others: Harriet Tubman, Gandhi, and Martin Luther King, who sought to liberate others from slavery and oppression; Albert Schweitzer and Simone Weil; but also the nonreligious Oskar Schindler and other rescuers of Jews in Nazi Europe, who placed their own lives in danger. Unless we assume that such individuals were *really* motivated by a narcissistic desire for glory or the avoidance of guilt, then we must conclude that the love of humanity is a realizable attitude and an original motivation for human behavior. And in spite of the cynical objections of critics such as Nietzsche and Freud, we must accept that the love of humanity cannot be reduced on every occasion to an underlying concern with ourselves.

From one perspective, then, the love of all humanity may be considered the highest fulfillment of love because it is the apparent telos of affectionate caring that begins within the family but then enlarges its scope to include one's peers and one's fellow citizens, until it embraces the whole of humanity itself. The love of humanity is guided by a concern and caring that grasps human beings as inherently valuable and important in themselves. Such a love is unconcerned with all specific differences such as religion, gender, race, and personal merit and focuses on the underlying sense in which all human beings are ultimately related to each other. In fact, it may be argued that the love of humanity is actually the most basic and authentic kind of love since it relates me to another person in an unconditional way, without consideration of my own private interests.

The philosophical basis for this kind of universal love is already present in ancient philosophy. It appears in the Stoic sense of humanity as a universal community bound by divine law to which as moral beings we must give our assent.[1] It can be found in Asian thought, in Mo Tzu, who argued that human love should be modeled on the will of heaven, which loves everyone equally; or in the figure of the Buddha, who refuses Nirvana until everyone has been redeemed from suffering.[2] Likewise, it is explicit in the Biblical commandment that one should love one's neighbor, and even one's enemy, as oneself. "This is my commandment," Jesus proclaims, "that you love one another as I have loved you." As the Gospel writers make clear, we cannot say that we truly love God unless we also love our neighbor.[3]

All of this history may be very compelling, and yet it may still be argued that the love of humanity is really insubstantial and very far from love's goal. If it is true that our experience of love originates in the family and gradually proceeds outward to include one's lovers, friends, and neighbors, then it follows that the love of humanity may actually be the weakest and most attenuated form of love, since it is furthest removed from the original passions from which it is derived. Freud argues along these lines in *Civilization and Its Discontents*, in which he claims that the love of humanity is often a form of escapism and a means of avoiding a real love relationship, which requires vulnerability and the possibility that one will be disappointed. He writes:

> A small minority are enabled by their constitution to find happiness, in spite of everything along the path of love. But these people make themselves independent of their object's acquiescence by displacing what they mainly value from being loved onto loving; they protect themselves against the loss of the object by directing their love, not to single objects but to all men alike; and they avoid the uncertainties and disappointments of genital love by turning away from its sexual aims and transforming the instinct into an impulse with an *inhibited aim*.[4]

Freud speculates that St. Francis of Assisi probably went as far as anyone in cultivating this approach to life. But he suggests that he was only able to achieve "a state of evenly suspended, steadfast, affectionate feeling, which has little external resemblance any more to the stormy agitations of genital love, from which it is nevertheless derived."[5] In what follows, Freud argues that such a love is unjust, and that not all men are worthy of love.

We might emphasize the inadequacy of such a love that in no way depends on the response of the beloved. To love someone, we might say, involves taking a risk and making oneself dependent on another person. If I really care about someone, then his or her desires and well-being will become important to me and at least partially constitutive of my own personal happiness. If I love you then I am subject to your rejection. And insofar as we are mutually involved with each other, our love is a reciprocal relationship that will transform both of us. But the love of humanity that Freud describes seems to lack any kind of personal involvement. And the "saint" that he depicts remains psychically aloof since he is able to incorporate any response, including indifference or rejection, as a test of his own "love," which endures no matter what.

From this perspective, the love of humanity is a rather debased form of love. And if we are inclined to accept that an authentic love relationship must involve an interaction between individuals who are transformed by their involvement with each other, then it may also follow that the love of humanity is not even an authentic form of loving. Freud argues that the love of humanity is a ruse and an attempt to avoid the emotional turbulence and entanglement that real love provides. Like Nietzsche in his comments on the Sermon on the Mount, he suggests that the love of humanity is really a "mask" for something else: specifically, weakness, or *ressentiment*, which cannot cope with the demands of personal life. Thus, far from being the fulfillment of love, the love of humanity may actually be motivated by a fear of involvement, or even disdain for particular individuals as such.

The early Christians were also disturbed by the apparent conflict between the universal goals of Christian love (or agape) and the particular attachments to friends and family that claimed them. If we want to mirror the love of God, can we ever be motivated by personal reasons or even give preference to one individual as opposed to another? When St. Augustine reflects back on his friendship with Nebridius, for example, he comes to the conclusion that such a love was wrong. "The grief I felt for the loss of my friend had struck so easily into my inmost heart," he writes, "simply because I had poured out my soul upon him, like water upon sand, loving a man who was mortal as though he were never to die."[6] The magnitude of St. Augustine's grief only underscores how excessive his love had been, and the lesson he draws from this points to the danger of particular attachments, which may distract us from the purer kind of love that agape represents. Kierkegaard also stresses the opposition between romantic love and neighbor love, and in his own life he felt obliged to sacrifice his relationship to Regina Olsen in order to remain close to God. Kierkegaard argues that friendship and romantic love are only partial loves insofar as they are based on our inclinations; in this regard, he claims, they are higher forms of self-love that allow us to enjoy our own ideal. By contrast, the love of humanity, or neighbor love, as he describes it, is unconditional since it is not motivated by our selfish concerns or in any way dependent on the neighbor's qualities.[7] This implies that if there *is* such a thing as the love of humanity it stands opposed to the other loves and cannot be viewed as their fulfillment. Or perhaps we should say that the other loves, such as friendship and romantic love, are only valid insofar as they bring us toward this privileged attitude of being.

This discussion shows that the love of humanity is the most ambiguous of all loves. At the same time that we must ask what the love of humanity is, we must also determine whether it really *is* a form of love. What is the value of this kind of love? Does humanitarian love stand in opposition to all of our particular loves, or should we say that the love of humanity—like the Christian agape—is actually the basis of love and the point of love's fulfillment?

In what follows, I begin by looking more closely at the Freudian perspective and Freud's argument against the possibility of universal love. In doing so, I really wish to examine the position that holds that human beings are basically selfish creatures, for this implies that the love of humanity is only *apparently* an other-regarding behavior, while in the end it is just another form of egoism. To show the inadequacy of this perspective will be to show that the love of humanity is an authentic form of love. But is this universal love *opposed* to all of the other loves, such as friendship and romantic love, that are focused on a particular other? And could it be that in order to experience the absolute love of humanity we have to abandon all of our particular attachments? To answer these questions, I look more closely at the Christian model of humanitarian love that is given in the interpretation of agape. In recent years, apologists and commentators have frequently insisted on the absolute difference between agape and eros as the forms of divine and human love. But in what sense can the divine model of love serve as a human ideal? The critique of agape, as it has been traditionally understood, will help to illuminate the real structure of humanitarian love and may suggest a continuity in the different forms of love and not an essential opposition or a hierarchy.

In conclusion, I try to describe the "place" in human desire and understanding from which the love of humanity is derived. Looking specifically at the rescuers of Jews in Nazi Europe, such a deep and selfless concern for others seems to reflect and affirm a particular way of thinking about our relationship to the human community. I do not believe that the love of humanity is only possible if one presupposes a religious framework, but that the love of humanity can be grasped as the expression of a "metaphysical" or "religious" attitude toward the world, where the latter is intended in a nontheological sense.

The Possibility of Univeral Love

Every human being must *learn* how to love. We are not born with an original sense of affection and caring for others. Rather, this is something that we acquire through our own experience of human society and the ways in which others interact with us and fulfill our needs. Thus, we may have an *innate* capacity to love, but this is something that must be nurtured. If we are not given appropriate models of love in our formative years, then our own love life and our ability to love will be seriously affected.

In his writings, Freud characterizes the state of infancy as one of "primary narcissism." He argues that before the infant has developed a sense of its own separate being in relation to others, it is literally self-absorbed and only aware of the world as a function of its own desires and needs. The loving attention of parents may help to prolong this narcissistic state, for parents "are under a compulsion to ascribe every perfection to the child—which sober observation would find no occasion to do—and to conceal and forget all his shortcomings."[8] As we grow up, however, we become increasingly aware of our own limitations and our dependence on others. And so it is hardly surprising that our parents should be the first objects of our love, since they are usually the ones who feed and protect us, and in loving them we are really exercising the instinct of self-preservation. In his essay "On Narcissism," Freud claims that each of our later "object-choices" in love may be understood either as an attempt to reproduce the original relationship with a parent by finding someone who will care for us in a similar way or as an attempt to recover the original condition of narcissism by loving and identifying with someone who seems to project an aura of self-sufficiency and containment. "We may say that a human being has originally two sexual objects," he writes, "himself and the woman who nurses him—and in doing so we are postulating a primary narcissism in everyone, which may in some cases manifest itself in a dominating fashion in his object-choice."[9]

Of course, Freud's discussion is a lot more nuanced than the brief account I have just described. But assuming that this reading is still more or less correct, Freud's argument appears to be quite speculative even at this point. We could argue just as easily, for example, that our original condition is one of helplessness and distress rather than "narcissism," which suggests self-absorption, enjoyment, and delight. Given the irrecoverable nature of psychological origins, why should we not endorse anxiety as our primary condition? It also seems to be axiomatic, and hence indisputable for Freud, that all love involves an unconscious attempt to recapture or reexperience the past, which means that in all of our later relationships with others we are doomed to repeat the original relationship with one's mother, father, or self. In a sense this is true, but only minimally: Previous loving attachments will always help to shape present and future ones. But to say that they determine all of our future relationships is a much bigger claim that cannot be proved with the evidence that Freud gives.

Even more questionable, however, is Freud's underlying claim that our love and affection for others is in every case derived from egoistic or narcissistic needs. Beginning with our first attachments, it might appear that all our love is self-interested in some way; this implies that altruism is just an extension of self-love. But having framed the issue in this way, when Freud goes on to speculate on the origins and goals of civilization, it seems obvious to him that we must relate the progress of civilization to our own original needs. And so it becomes true by definition that every human community and every loving impulse, including the love of humanity, must ultimately relate to our own self-love. If we must sacrifice the possibility of immediate gratification, then this can only be for a more compelling long-term gain that is also self-regarding; in this way, the whole of civilization becomes a ruse for achieving our own ends. Now according to Freud, the problem is that we have now reached a point at which the advantages of civilization are in profound conflict with the instinctual renunciation that civilization requires. He speculates pessimistically that we are fast reaching the point at which civilization may have "outlived" itself, since it is no longer in our own best interests and actually produces more misery than it was supposed to prevent. "If civilization is a necessary course of development from the family to humanity as a whole," he comments, "then, as a result of the inborn conflict arising from ambivalence, of the eternal struggle between the trends of love and death—there is inextricably bound up with it an increase of the sense of guilt, which will perhaps reach heights that the individual finds hard to tolerate."[10] We may or may not accept Freud's discussion of the history of civilization. The important point is that there is a strong sense in which his analysis is flawed, because he assumes something about human nature that still remains unproven.

Like many other thinkers, Freud apparently assumes that everything that we do must be motivated by self-interest of one kind or another; if this is the case, then pure altruism is an absurd possibility. Thus, when he discusses love in the early pages of *Civilization and Its Discontents*, he describes it from this perspective, along with the life of action or the contemplation of beauty, as one of the main ways in which individuals attempt to achieve happiness for themselves in life:

A psychical attitude of this sort comes naturally enough to all of us. Indeed, one of the forms in which love manifests itself—sexual love—has given us our most intense experience of an overwhelming sensation of pleasure and has thus furnished us with a pattern for our search for happiness. What is more natural than that we should persist in looking for happiness along the path on which we first encountered it?

But then he comments, quite cogently: "The weak side of this technique of living is easy to see. . . . It is that we are never so defenseless against suffering as when we love, never so helplessly unhappy as when we have lost our loved object or its love."[11] Here it is taken for granted that the ego will always project a certain path for itself in order to secure personal happiness, and that love, although intense, does not always guarantee a successful result. It follows from this that the love of all humanity may be viewed as a strategic response to this difficulty, since it allows one to have the fulfillment of love without the possibility of disappointment. As we have seen, Freud considers St. Francis as the classic exemplar of this kind of love because he directed his affection onto all creatures, both human and nonhuman alike, and thereby protected himself against the possibility of loss that attachment to a single object must bring.

Freud is insightful on a number of points, but this whole argument really begs the question because it assumes that the nature of love must always be determined by the original conditions of its emergence. It also presupposes that the egoistic needs that prevail in infancy will continue to infect our love, so that even the most spiritually developed individual must be directed by self-regarding desires. This argument assumes that the basic nature of the self remains the same over the course of one's life and implies that every kind of love has the same origin in the subject's libido, though sometimes it will be gratified and sometimes it will be "aim inhibited." I think that Freud, and more generally this whole way of thinking about love, is wrong on both counts, and in a moment I will explain why.

Once again, however, Freud's position is a lot more complex than this brief discussion suggests. So far, it would appear that for Freud all of our love is either self-interested and a veiled form of egoism or else destructive to the ego, so that in loving another we are actually diminishing our own power. When he describes the excesses of erotic love, for example, he points out the great danger of romantic obsession and infatuation. He argues that we must experience depletion and low self-esteem whenever we project our ego ideal completely outside of ourselves and onto another. But the very discussion of this pathological case suggests that there is also a corresponding norm, a healthy form of romantic involvement that does not entail self-abandonment. Likewise, we may point out that even though Freud often dwells on the conflictual nature of human relationships, such as the (male) child's Oedipal development against his father, it is important to remember his claim that this struggle is usually resolved in the process of identifying with the other, in this case the father. And so, from our existence as isolated beings, we gradually experience a growing sense of community with our family, our friends, and the nation itself, usually in the form of patriotism in national defense. As Freud puts it, "Civilization is a process in the service of Eros, whose purpose is to combine single human individuals, and after that families, then races, peoples and nations into one great unity, the unity of mankind. Why this has to happen, we do not know; the work of Eros is precisely this. These collections of men are to be libidinally bound to one another."[12]

Now this is important, because it suggests that in opposition to what Freud implies elsewhere, the identity that we have is something that grows and develops through our association with others. Instead of remaining inherently selfish and self-regarding beings, there is reason to believe that our personal identity is actually transformed or clarified by our loving relationships with other people in such a way that their personal interests become a part of our own. And so it becomes impossible in this model to distinguish what concerns me personally from what concerns my loved ones, my family and my friends. Love, I have suggested, implies at least to some extent the sharing of identities in the sense that what matters to my loved ones will be something that matters to me. This is why self-sacrifice is possible, because I do have a shared sense of belonging with others. Their interests can become just as important to me as my own, to the extent that I can no longer distinguish a separate sense of what would be good for me as opposed to what would be good for them. And so if I make a "sacrifice" for my child or my friend, I usually do not regard it in this light. I have no choice; it is something that I have to do. And now the question can be raised, Could we ever identify so completely with humanity itself that we could experience universal love for all of humankind?

Let us now return to the case of Freud's lover of all humanity who finds happiness, "in spite of everything, along the path of love." In *Civilization and Its Discontents*, Freud argues that even if the love of all humanity were possible, it would remain a very insipid kind of love since it would have to be spread so thinly. "But if I am to love him [with this universal love]" he writes, "merely because he, too, is an inhabitant of this earth, like an insect, an earth-worm or a grass-snake, then I fear that only a small modicum of my love will fall to his share—not by any possibility as much as, by the judgement of my reason, I am entitled to retain for myself."[13] Freud also argues that such a love would actually be unjust, for in amplifying our love for everyone else, we would have less love available for those who are closest to us and hence deserve it more. Both of these arguments may be challenged, however, since they rely on a false premise that assimilates the generosity and the proliferation of love to the limited economy of the libido—as if there could only ever be a fixed amount of love in circulation at any one time. This denies the common experience that in love "to divide is not [necessarily] to take away."[14] If I have two children, I do not have to love either one of them any *less* than if I only had one, and the effect of a loving relationship is usually to make me more rather than less loving to others.

Nevertheless, Freud is right to challenge the specific model of humanitarian love that he describes. He argues that such a love is a ruse and a way of avoiding the risks of normal love while still apparently loving. Nietzsche makes similar claims against humanitarian love by suggesting that the love of humanity is motivated by self-hatred or by a desire for vengeance against all that is powerful and strong, and that one hurries to one's neighbor and the life of the community in order to escape from oneself.[15] Similarly, when the saint turns deliberately toward the weak and the oppressed of the earth, it may well be the case that he cherishes them since they are exactly opposite to the powerful ones that he despises. In his book *Ressentiment*, Max Scheler attempts to distinguish between two types of love that he claims are often confused. Scheler tries to defend Christianity from Nietzsche's charges, but at the same time he endorses the critique of modern humanitarian love as a form of self-hatred and flight:

> One cannot love anybody without turning away from oneself. However, the crucial question is whether this movement is prompted by the desire to turn toward a positive value, or whether the intention is a radical escape from oneself. "Love" of the second variety is inspired by self-hatred, by hatred of one's own weakness and misery. The mind is always on the point of departing for distant places. Afraid of seeing itself and its inferiority, it is driven to give

itself to the other—not because of his worth, but merely for the sake of his "otherness." Modern philosophical jargon has found a revealing term for this phenomenon, one of the many modern substitutes for love: "altruism." This love is not directed at a previously discovered positive value, nor does any such value flash up in the act of loving: there is nothing but the urge to turn away from oneself and to lose oneself in other people's business."[16]

We can ignore Scheler's rancor against modernity as a form of the very *ressentiment* that he describes. What is significant here, though, is that both he and Nietzsche before him emphasize the respect in which "love" can always be a front for something else. Even if we claim to love someone or something, there is still the deeper question as to whether our manifest devotion is empowered by something other than love, such as the desire for possession or the hatred of oneself.

In the case of the example that Freud uses, the person who makes himself independent of his object's acquiescence "by displacing what [he] mainly value[s] from being loved onto loving," there is a strong suggestion that something other than love is being described. To determine what is wrong here, we must now provide an authentic model of humanitarian love that would illuminate the deficiency of the model that Freud considers. In fact, our intuitions should tell us that there is something wrong with a love that remains so totally unaffected by what it loves. As I have suggested, the real problem with the kind of love that Freud describes is that it is not reciprocal. It gives the impression of a remote subject who holds the other at a distance like a separate object, while remaining inviolate and basically uninvolved. But it is clear that loving someone must always involve a strong possibility of self-transformation. Insofar as I love you, I am in some way identifying your interests as mine, and I am not closed off from you but open to the possibility of being affected by you. In what sense would I really "love" someone if I remained self-sufficient and out of play? Freud's passage does not describe a genuine case of humanitarian love. It is at best an example of benevolence that is indefinitely extended, but since it remains so totally under the control of the subject, as a part of his fixed identity, it cannot be described as "love." Love requires involvement with the beloved and reciprocity, which means that it must be a transformative experience for the lover as well as the beloved. To claim that one loves someone and yet to remain unaffected by her would seem to be a contradiction in terms, for love requires responsiveness to the beloved, and the experience of her needs as being important as one's own. If one were unaffected by the beloved, that would imply that her desires and needs remained irrelevant to oneself.

The real problem with the love of humanity is that it seems to be a very nonspecific form of love, in which the object of concern is at the same time both everyone and no one in particular. Perhaps, as Hume argues, there is an underlying "benevolence" that forms an essential part of our makeup, even though this is frequently obscured by more immediately selfish concerns.[17] But even if we accept this, it still does not explain how it is possible for anyone to really love an abstraction, such as "humanity in general," since loving requires involvement, and involvement presupposes a very particular knowledge and an awareness of those whom one loves. Hence it is possible to love particular individuals, and the more we know about them the more we will be able to respond to them with appropriate loving attention. If I have several children, I will respond to each of them differently, taking care to learn about each one of them and the particular ways in which I can nurture them. But it would certainly be a mistake to try to love all of my children in exactly the same way. Love requires a particular attention to the beloved, who is to be valued for his or her own sake. And this means that the beloved cannot be viewed as a simple unit of humanity who must be cared for like everyone else. Again, in a romantic context, "love" without any particular knowledge is equivalent to infatuation, or "enthusiasm" in a bad sense—which is a self-regarding passion that either becomes genuine love as the lover comes to know the beloved or else disappears.

There is definitely a difficulty, then, with the very idea of a "love" that does not relate to particular individuals who are to be cherished and valued for themselves, for love in its very essence is focused on the specificity of the beloved. Freud's mistake is to think of the love of humanity and the love of a particular individual in entirely oppositional terms. Indeed, for Freud, the love of humanity seems to be premised on the avoidance of particular affections, and this is very problematic. Perhaps in some cases what passes as humanitarian love is actually a cover for the rejection of other people, but it would be more reasonable to think of the two levels of love, in their most authentic forms, as being reciprocally related to each other. Thus, it is my sense of belonging to all humankind, my species being as it were, that makes it possible for me to love and cherish particular others and to recognize that since we all share the same basic needs we should all be cherished; conversely, in loving a particular person I also open myself up to the possibility of loving and cherishing all other people, regardless of my actual relation to them, and in this way my love of humanity is strengthened and inspired. Along similar lines, Freud's paradox can be resolved once we accept that in loving and caring for the stranger, with whom we have no personal ties, we are thereby loving and affirming the whole of humanity itself. To put this another way, the love of humanity is only possible if it can be achieved within a particular loving relationship and not as an indifferent projection onto all.

The story of the good Samaritan, for example, describes the loving response of one individual to another who suffers and needs help. At the outset, the Samaritan knows nothing about the wounded man, and he has no particular reason to help him. But insofar as he cares for him, he values his life, he makes it his business to determine what the wounded man needs, and he gives him appropriate help:

> A man was going down from Jerusalem to Jericho, and he fell among robbers, who stripped him and beat him, and departed, leaving him half dead. Now by chance a priest was going down that road; and when he saw him he passed by on the other side. So likewise a Levite, when he came to the place and saw him, passed by on the other side. But a Samaritan, as he journeyed, came to where he was; and when he saw him he had compassion, and went to him and bound up his wounds, pouring on oil and wine; then he set him on his own beast and brought him to an inn, and took care of him. And the next day he took out two denarii and gave them to the innkeeper saying, "Take care of him; and whatever more you spend, I will repay when I come back."[18]

This is an example of the love of humanity, or neighbor love, as the Gospels describe it. The whole point of the story is the loving concern of the Samaritan, who responded to the wounded man simply as a human being. He did not first determine whether the victim was someone he knew or whether he was someone of the same religious faith; he did not even consider whether it would be safe or fitting to help him. In a profound sense, the parable describes the pure generosity and availability of one individual to another, without mediation and without reserve and without any ulterior motive, including the desire for salvation. Likewise, the Samaritan does not help the man on the side of the road because the latter belongs to the class of poor or wretched people. Although this would be an example of justice, it would not be love, which requires a caring involvement with the other person for his own sake. And while the Samaritan may know nothing about the other person to begin with, this is something that he goes beyond since the conditions of love require it.

Similarly, Oskar Schindler is rightly hailed as a moral hero for saving the lives of hundreds of Jews during World War II. But it would certainly be very misleading to say that all of his efforts were inspired by a universal love of humanity on the Freudian model. Quite apart from his allegiance to any particular principle, Schindler responded to the specific needs of the men and women that he helped. According to one survivor, everyone had his or her own story about Schindler and thought that Schindler's concern for them was somehow unique. One woman needed a pair of glasses and he found some for her; another woman had a son in Poland, and Schindler found a way to bring messages from him; a third was sick in the infirmary and all she wanted was an apple, and Schindler brought her one.[19] Toward the end of the war, several trainloads of Schindler's Jews were mistakenly sent to Auschwitz. As a simple altruist he could presumably have accepted a new consignment of Jews to replace those he had lost. But what mattered to him was not humankind in the abstract or the saving of so many units of humanity, but the Jews that he had sheltered, and he made every effort to recover them. Insofar as he cared for these people that he saved, Schindler opened himself to them and made their fate and their own personal distress something that mattered to him.

Love implies an active involvement with another and the continuing possibility of self-transformation that such a relationship involves. In the case of the love of humanity, however, there is no single object called "humanity" that we can have a particular involvement with. But this does not mean, as Freud supposes, that the love of humanity is really fraudulent. On the contrary, in the case of the good Samaritan or the rescuers of Jews in the Holocaust, the love of humanity is expressed in very determinate ways. And such a love, like all love, requires an emotional involvement with the other person, a background of compassion as well as a particular knowledge of the beloved and a willingness to act on his or her behalf. Egoistic accounts of love and morality seem to miss the point here, since it *is* possible to have another person's happiness as one's interest and to strive for his or her well-being even when this may be at great cost to oneself. But this does not involve any hidden motivation, for to love another, even a stranger, implies that we no longer make such a strict distinction between our own interests and those of someone else. To put this differently: If another person's needs are important to me, then this can only be because at some level I recognize the other as someone who is related to me. I experience a shared sense of belonging in the same way that I would in belonging to a particular family— and this becomes an important aspect of who I am. In many ways, the child is related to her parents as an extension of their own identity. Likewise, the friend, at least according to Aristotle, is a second self. And in responding to the stranger who claims me, I am driven by a recognition of our shared humanity, which transcends our differences and which may still exist even if he is supposed to be my enemy.

Freud's attack on the love of humanity proves useful, then, if only because it helps us to distinguish between the inauthentic and abstract love that he describes and the positive version of humanitarian love that must be contrasted with it. One of the most significant aspects of love is that it has the power to transform and enlarge our own sense of self and our personal identity, and the love of humanity is certainly no exception. In fact, the love of humanity expresses the most complete reorientation of the individual, away from the selfish ego that Freud describes and toward an acceptance of oneself as someone who belongs to the whole of humanity. The active expression of this love testifies to this sense of belonging, which can become the most important thing to an individual. Some, such as Schweitzer or Schindler, have been ready to sacrifice themselves for it.

In Christianity, the love of one's neighbor is specifically required, although the latter is not the abstraction that Freud so rightly condemns. Having shown the possibility of humanitarian love and the form it might involve, let us now turn to the specifically Christian concept of love (or agape). Agape is historically important as an attempt to describe and commend the love of humanity insofar as the latter may also be viewed as the fulfillment of the individual life. We may decide that as the image of divine love, agape remains an impossible paradigm, and so it may not be suitable for human beings to aspire to. Or we may still regard it as a goal that can motivate our behavior and inspire us toward it. The main issue here is whether agape or the love of humanity must be sharply distinguished from the other forms of love—as Freud and many Christian commentators claim—or whether the different forms of love are finally continuous with each other.

Agape and Eros

In describing the history of love, it is now quite customary to draw a sharp distinction between the Greek account of eros and the Christian model of agape because at first glance these two ideals of love seem to have a completely different structure and goal.[20] Thus it could be argued that for the Greeks, love is based on need and a sense of our own incompleteness. According to Plato, love is the child of poverty and artifice. But in this respect, it is also the power that takes us out of ourselves and keeps us yearning for that which is higher and better. In the *Symposium*, Diotima describes a ladder of love that begins with the love of individual beauty and leads all the way to the vision of absolute Beauty. "This is what it is to go aright," she says, "or be led by another into the mystery of love; one goes always upwards for the sake of this Beauty"; and, "If someone got to see the Beautiful itself, absolute, pure, unmixed, not polluted by human flesh or colours or any other great non-sense of mortality, if he could see the divine Beauty itself in its one form do you think it would be a poor life for a human being to look there and to behold it and to be with it."[21] Hence eros—or at least the good eros—is totally bound up with self-fulfillment and perfectibility. The goal of this spiritual progress, the realm of the eternal and the Good, remains completely self-sufficient and self-contained, like Aristotle's unmoved mover or the gods who cannot be overwhelmed by love because they are already perfect, or like Socrates, who strives relentlessly to approach this divine order of being and who is consequently self-controlled and the master of his passions. Socrates remains unmoved by Alcibiades' physical charms because he has already gone so much further than the love of physical beauty in his own pursuit of the good. "Dear Alcibiades," he says, "if you are right in what you say about me, you are already more accomplished than you think. If I really have in me the power to make you a better man, then you can see in me a beauty that is really beyond description and makes your own remarkable good looks pale in comparison. But, then, is this a fair exchange that you propose? You seem to me to want more than your proper share: you offer me the merest appearance of beauty, and in return you want the thing itself, 'gold in exchange for bronze.'"[22]

All of this is very different from Christianity, in which God is portrayed as infinitely merciful and loving. In fact, it is said that "God is love," and out of love for the world he sent his only son to die for our sins. The life of Jesus emphasizes personal sacrifice and devotion to others, and it is said that he came not only for the good but also and especially for the sinners and the worst kind of men and women, who are most needful of help. In the case of Christianity, then, it seems that love cannot simply be equated with Greek ideals of self-actualization and improvement. The divine does not represent the telos of love but the site of love's emergence, and it is held that insofar as we love another in a Christian way we thereby participate in the nature of Christ. "This is my commandment," Jesus proclaims, "that you love one another as I have loved you."[23] In the first letter of John, this is justified and explained: "Beloved, let us love one another; for love is of God, and he who knows is born of God and knows God. He who does not love does not know God; for God is love."[24] And again, "if we love one another, God abides in us and his love is perfected in us."[25] Over the years, many scholars and theologians have argued that Christianity enjoins a very particular kind of love. In the New Testament, *agape* is the word that is most often used. This is usually translated as "charity" or the love of one's neighbor, but it cannot be reduced to friendship or any other love that is motivated by the particular qualities of the beloved. Theologians since St. Paul have sought to clarify the precise nature of agape, and they have tried to resolve some of the apparent problems that arise when a divine example of love is viewed as the appropriate model for human beings to follow.

Jesus says that the whole of the law can be reduced to the following: "You shall love the Lord your God with all your heart, and with all your soul, and with all your strength, and with all your mind; and your neighbor as yourself."[26] It is the latter theme that concerns us, where one's "neighbor" is understood to be *anyone*, without regard to whether we have any special ties or responsibilities to him or her. Our relationships to our nearest and dearest, our friends, family, and lovers, are founded on mutual concern and moral commitment. But when Jesus commands us to love our neighbors, he seems to intend that we must also care for strangers and for those who cannot make any special claims on us. Regardless of our own religious beliefs, much of our ethical thinking and our experience of other people has already been conditioned by this Christian account of love. And it is this that we need to articulate and make explicit, to determine whether the concept remains appropriate to the experience of this kind of love.

In the New Testament, Jesus does not present theories or sustained philosophical arguments to clarify his teachings or help his listeners understand. For the most part, he teaches through the illustration of parables. And while this still leaves a lot of room for interpretation, if we want to understand agape this would probably be the best place to begin. We have already referred to the parable of the good Samaritan, which gives us an example of an unconditional love and caring for another person. The Samaritan did not know the victim on the side of the road—whether he was important or another Samaritan, or whether the latter would have helped him if their situations had been reversed. Likewise, he did not have to help him: Two others had already passed by on the other side of the street. But he obviously felt compassion and concern, and in helping the stranger he had no other consideration than what was best for this unfortunate man. If we assume the rational self-interested view of human nature, then there would be no good reason for the Samaritan to stop and help. To suggest that he might be acting for the sake of some future religious reward seems a bit speculative and unlikely in this context. The Samaritan does not make any kind of a calculation. He simply responds to the victim, who needs protection and caring. And this response is presented as the paradigm of what "loving one's neighbor" means.

On another occasion, Jesus tells the parable of the prodigal son, which further extends our understanding of agape. A man had two sons. The younger son asked his father for his share of the property in advance, and then he went abroad and squandered all of his money on loose living. There was a terrible famine, and the younger son was reduced to feeding pigs in order to survive. He reflected that even his father's servants were much better off than he was, and so he decided to return home, ask for his father's forgiveness, and beg for a job as a hired hand. When he is still far off, the father sees him and rejoices. He runs out to embrace his wayward son, and he tells his servants to kill the fatted calf to celebrate his return. But the elder son is angry and unhappy and refuses to come in: "Lo, these many years I have served you," he tells his father, "and I have never disobeyed your command; yet you never gave me a kid that I might make merry with my friends." In reply, the father says, "Son, you are always with me and all that is mine is yours." He adds that it was only fitting to celebrate his son's return, "for he was lost, and is found."[27]

Given the overall context of this parable, it seems fairly clear that in this case the loving and forgiving father is meant to refer to God. His loving attitude toward his son is affirmed, and so our own initial impulse to condemn the prodigal son, or anyone who squanders what they have been given, must be overcome. Even if the latter is not entitled to anything in the name of justice, he must still be cared for with compassion and love, even to the point of celebration. The older son is annoyed by his father's response and stays away. He feels he has earned the right to all he has, whereas his brother has already had his share. It is this narrow and unforgiving attitude that is condemned here, even though it seems to have the principle of justice behind it. In fact, this parable is very straightforward in the way that it puts justice and love in apparent opposition to each other. This is not to say that charity is never coextensive with the requirements of justice. Indeed, it seems quite likely that Jesus's special preference for the poor and the dispossessed is also motivated by a concern for justice and a desire to help those who have not had the advantages others enjoyed. The important point here is that the love of humanity, or agape, that this parable expresses must be much more than the concern for justice that is presumably the second brother's standpoint.

The parable of the prodigal son, together with others such as the good Samaritan or the laborers in the vineyard, tends to emphasize that agape is an absolutely generous love, even excessive at times, which is given without calculation or the expectation of a return. For a Christian, the life of Jesus expresses the same loving generosity. In this respect, we may understand agape as the passionate concern for the life and well-being of another that does not depend on the objective value or the worthiness of those who are cared for—in the case of the Samaritan this was unknown, and in the case of the prodigal son the individual did not really "deserve" anything, let alone the fatted calf. Agape flows from the "goodness" of the Samaritan and the father in responding to the other's needs and in taking the other as someone who is absolutely worth caring for.

The traditional opposition between agape and eros is apparently confirmed here. For even if eros is directed toward a higher good, as opposed to an individual beauty, it is still a self-regarding impulse, albeit of a nobler sort, whereas agape is directed toward the other person and cherishes her for her sake alone. But is it really possible to maintain such a strict separation between a love that is ultimately self-regarding and another that is really focused on the other? Of course, I want my friend to succeed, but that is not simply another aspect of my own egoism but an aspect of my love for my friend, and it is him that I am concerned about rather than myself. Similarly, the Samaritan showed love and compassion for the beaten stranger, and while the most important thing was simply to get him some help, in loving and caring for the stranger he is able to affirm his own sense of relation and belonging to humanity itself. What this suggests is that the distinction between mine and thine begins to break down at a certain point, especially if we accept that personal identity is defined in terms of our relation to particular others as well as in terms of our relation to the community or even humankind in general. Let us keep this point in mind while we briefly consider C. S. Lewis and Anders Nygren on this theme.

In *The Four Loves*, C. S. Lewis begins his discussion by distinguishing between "need love," such as friendship and romantic love, which is based on a lack that we need to fill, and "gift love," which comes, he claims, from superabundance and joy in wanting to give. Lewis regards all of the varieties of need love as preliminary to agape, or the divine bestowal of love. In fact, he says, "The ultimate value of the other love is to prepare us for agape," which he claims is the eternal element in one's love for someone.[28] In making an evaluative comparison between the different kinds of love, C. S. Lewis is following a strong tendency of Christian thinking that regards the earthly affections and heavenly love as in conflict with each other. From one point of view, earthly loves are ultimately superseded or given their place by agape, which has perhaps supported them all along. From another point of view, any deep affection for a particular other is ultimately a distraction from the love of God and neighbor, and so we are bound to choose between them. Both perspectives find the relationship between agape and the other loves to be deeply problematic; this is perhaps inescapable if we represent agape as a heavenly love (even if it is sometimes mediated through loving one's neighbor) and eros and philia as loves that keep us bound to worldly things. What I want to suggest, however, is that from a "humanistic" and this-worldly perspective, the love of humanity that agape expresses is really not so discontinuous with erotic love and friendship. As I suggested at the outset, it makes sense to assume that a successful development in one kind of love leads us to become more generous in our loving and more capable of embracing humanity itself. Of course, we may become obsessive or fixated in our romantic affections, but this would be an unhealthy form of romantic involvement, and it would not follow that every case of romantic involvement is ultimately self-destructive in this way. Likewise, one could also be so concerned with the plight of others that one's own nearest and dearest would suffer. It seems obvious, in fact, that if we are happy and fulfilled in our personal loves and friendships then we will be much more open and available to others, and much more willing to give of ourselves. This suggests the real continuity of all our love, including the love of humanity itself.

In his famous discussion of the absolute difference between agape and eros, Anders Nygren argues that "eros and agape are the characteristic expressions of two different attitudes to life, two fundamentally opposed types of religion and ethics. They represent two streams that run through the whole history of religion, alternately clashing against one another and mingling with one another." Despite their historical involvement with each other, however, Nygren argues that they are antagonistic and completely antithetical attitudes: "There seems in fact to be no possibility of discovering any idea common to them both which might serve as the starting-point for the comparison; for at every point the opposition between them makes itself felt."[29]

I think we have good reason to be suspicious whenever authors describe an opposition or a distinction between two different modalities as so absolute and unbridgeable. Indeed, they usually support the absolute priority of one term in the opposition, which, on closer inspection, is found to rely on the other. Our philosophical experience tells us that divisions like this one cannot usually be sustained. At this point, though, we can reach a more profound understanding of the love of humanity if we just consider Nygren's most basic claims about agape, and the problems that follow from his focus upon *God's* love, as opposed to the love of humanity.

In *Agape and Eros*, Nygren describes the four most important features of agape as follows. First, he claims that "agape is spontaneous and unmotivated."[30] God had no reason to create the world or to send his son to save us. In no sense was he obliged to act or motivated by the personal goodness of men and women or their inherent value. In the end, God's excessive love is just an expression of his own perfect and loving nature: It is in no way dependent on us and whether we are worth loving. Second, to emphasize this point, Nygren claims that "agape is indifferent to value." In contrast to the classical conception of eros, which recognizes value in something higher and aspires toward it, agape is in no way directed toward individuals on account of their merits, their right-eousness, or their goodness, for this would be to make God's love conditional and constrained. God's love is directed toward the righteous and sinners alike. Third, Nygren argues that agape is creative love. God does not recognize something or someone as inherently valuable, but insofar as he loves it he bestows value on it. Thus Nygren insists that the human being has no value *unless* he or she is loved by God, and he condemns the teaching that upholds "the infinite value of the human soul." He claims this is mistaken since it would make God's love conditional and moti-vated after all. Finally, Nygren argues that "agape is the imitator of fellowship with God." Only agape can establish ties between the human and the divine. It follows from this that we cannot come to God by ourselves. Only agape can bring us to him; but although we may participate in agape by loving God or loving our neighbor, it is still the case that agape ultimately derives from God, and he is responsible for it.

Even though this summary has focused on the nature of God's love for us as opposed to our love for our neighbor, it can still be examined and assessed as the model for altruistic loving. I am not concerned with the theological problems of Nygren's position. If God is the only real agent of agape, for example, then it would seem to follow that even when we do love him, he is only loving himself through us—which implies that in the end we are merely the passive recipients of God's agency and can never initiate any-thing by ourselves. Likewise, if God's love is a pure spontaneity that is indifferent to its object, then it would also follow that God is actually indifferent to our response. It is not clear how the theolo-gian should respond to difficulties like these. This leads us to ques-tion the extent to which the "supernatural" account of agape could ever serve as an appropriate model for neighbor love. Leaving these debates to one side, however, let us now return to the four basic points of Nygren's analysis to determine the strengths and weaknesses of this particular reading of agape as something that human beings can enjoy. The discussion will bring us to some final conclusions concerning the love of humanity and its relation to the other loves.

The first claim is that agape is "spontaneous and unmotivated." To counter the obvious objection that such a love must therefore be quite arbitrary, Nygren argues that in the case of God, at least, it is simply the inevitable expression of his essential nature. But unless we assume without question that God must be working through us when we love our neighbor, this does not really help us to explain humanitarian love. In one sense, of course, "unmotivated" suggests "for no selfish reason." But it also implies "uncaused," and in the latter sense the very idea of an unmotivated love would seem to be a contradiction. As we saw when we considered Freud's lover of humanity, love is not an unchanging force that can be directed toward anything or anyone while remaining unaffected by its object. I do not love my child in the same way that I love my friend, because my friend and my child are very different individuals that I must respond to in very different ways. Indeed, since no two people are identical, it may also be the case that no two people may be loved in exactly the same way. What this suggests is that the love of humanity is not "spontaneous" but is to a very great extent conditioned by the specific needs and desires of the ones to whom we must respond. We need to know what our neighbor needs—help, encouragement, or food—and the ways in which we can best encourage him or her to prosper and thrive. And this means that to love someone requires that we try to know that person as well as we can, to learn about his or her life as well as we can, and to respond appropriately to him or her.

The second claim is that agape is "indifferent to value." In the context of God's love for human beings, this means that God loves all of us alike, saints as well as sinners, without regard to whether we really deserve this love or not. In one respect, this emphasizes the absolute forgiveness and acceptance that God offers us, like a parent whose love for his children is completely unconditional. This view is quite helpful: I have just argued that humanitarian love must be focused on the needs and desires of the other. And since such a love is not conditional on my own private needs, it would be indifferent to—in the sense of being unaffected by—the neighbor's personal merit or the lack of it. On the other hand, such love, like all love, must be directed toward the actual or the possible good in the one who is cared for. If I visit a criminal in prison, I may show him caring and love, not because he is a criminal who has created suffering and misery, but in spite of these things. I see the good in him or the potential for good that he has as a human being. And as I learn more about him, I will try to help him by encouraging his good qualities and suggesting possible ways in which he could continue to grow. In this sense, love, including humanitarian love, must idealize its object. It always fastens on to what is valuable and good, and it projects the possibility of the good as something that may be achieved. In this respect, the love of humanity is not indifferent to value, but like all love is focused on the proximity of the beloved to the good.

This brings us to the third point: "Agape is creative," which means that insofar as God loves us he makes us valuable. According to Nygren, God does not respond to our own inherent value since we really have none. We are only valuable because God loves us, and in this respect the bestowal of love is the origin of all value. Now, there is a sense in which we can relate to this: At one level, love *is* a creative activity because it illuminates the beloved's potential and allows him or her to become a better person. If someone loves me, then I am more likely to think of myself as a valuable being who is capable of much; if I am not loved, then it will be harder for me to recognize my own worth. At the same time, however, there is something wrong with insisting on the *purely* creative aspects of such loving. When I love someone and actively care for her, it means that I am concerned for her well-being. I value what is good for her precisely because it is good *for her,* and not because what is good for her is ultimately good for me. When I love and care for someone, even if this is a stranger who needs my help, it is as if I were saying, "You are absolutely valuable." By this I mean "You are valuable and therefore I love you," but not "You are valuable because I love you," for the latter would make love into a form of self-regard. In this respect, love involves both the bestowal of value and the recognition of value, for without the latter love would be superfluous and arbitrary. An excess of loving feelings projected onto someone else does not constitute love. Loving begins when we can respond to another person and are able to experience his or her own desires and needs as being as important as our own.

The final point about agape is that it provides for fellowship with God. Depending on our own religious preferences, we may choose to affirm this claim as literally true or we may view it symbolically, in the sense that such a love is the fulfillment of human life and allows us to overcome human isolation by putting us in touch with our greater identity with humanity as a whole. Of course, we do all we can for our nearest and dearest because they are, in some sense, extensions and reflections of ourselves. But in loving our neighbor—or in caring for a complete stranger—it is as if we were giving in a more absolute sense. Such a love is not arbitrary or spontaneous. It is a consequence of the fact that I experience a sense of belonging to a greater community than just my immediate circle—and this belonging is ultimately constitutive of my own personal identity and the sense of who I am. Likewise, this sense of belonging is not merely an intellectual recognition; it is an emotional involvement and identification that becomes a motive force in everything that I do.

In what follows, I focus on the rescuers of Jews in Nazi Europe, who were religious and nonreligious alike. I suggest that they were able to do what they did because they had a strong sense of their involvement with humanity as a whole, and I argue that this is where the love of humanity is ultimately derived. In the end, the specifically religious interpretation of agape has proved unhelpful. But in the course of this analysis and critique we have gained some confirmation of the structure of humanitarian love as a *human* possibility.

Rescuing Humanity

The discussion of love, and the love of humanity in particular, appears to call into question the absolute distinction between egoism and altruism as the two basic principles of human motivation. This is because love enlarges the scope of personal identity. To love someone else implies a deep involvement with that person, such that we experience that person's interest and well-being as if they were our own; indeed, the well-being of the beloved becomes constitutive of our own personal happiness, so that in the end it is rather artificial to separate the one from the other. In a sense, love involves the ability to step back from oneself, to focus one's attention on another person, and to recognize, in more than just an intellectual sense, that he or she is also the subject of a life and must be cherished and cared for.[31] But this does not mean that in every case "love" must involve some kind of self-abandonment and a flight from the everyday demands that are placed on the ego. This may be the case with some examples of romantic obsession that are ultimately founded on a self-regarding impulse, but if we return to the love of humanity, we are faced with a host of examples that cannot be explained in this manner.

During World War II, for example, most people in German-occupied territories did nothing to help local Jews, who were persecuted and eventually sent to death camps. They may have felt compassion for them, but given the might of the Nazis, they believed that there really was nothing they could do. Such behavior can very easily be explained, if not justified, in terms of rational self-interest. But at the same time, some individuals, such as the Trocmés in Le Chambon, Oskar Schindler, and others who are less well known, were ready to help Jews to escape or to hide them in their houses, even though they risked losing their own lives if they were ever caught. On the one hand, the rescuers of Jews were obviously not acting in the interests of their own personal survival and well-being. And it seems a real stretch to attribute their behavior to a need for celebrity, especially since they had to work in secret, and even after the war many of them were shunned. Nor is there a straightforward religious explanation for this: Pastor Trocmé helped, whereas some other clergy collaborated; Schindler and other rescuers had no religious beliefs. On the other hand, it is also unconvincing to claim that such devotion and caring for the lives of strangers was really an expression of self-abandonment and an inability to pursue what was ultimately beneficial for themselves. Most people did not help because they were indifferent or simply afraid. To run such tremendous risks, often for years and without the benefit of a supporting community, the rescuers, unlike the bystanders, had to have a very strong sense of personal identity that they expressed through the courage of their convictions, even in the face of death. The important point is that this identity actually involved a very deep sense of belonging and connectedness to other people and a refusal to consider that their own lives might be separate and unconcerned with those who were being persecuted or less fortunate than themselves.[32]

During the war years, Jews were persecuted, killed, and in every way deprived of their humanity and treated as if they were subhuman. By helping Jews, the rescuers were thereby affirming what the Nazis denied. The love of humanity that the rescuers displayed was thus a response to a specific circumstance, exactly like the example of the good Samaritan. But it was not simply a *moral* choice on their part, or a matter of weighing up the pros and the cons and reaching an ethical conclusion. In fact, when they describe their decision to help, rescuers invariably comment that they did not really have any choice in the matter. What else was one to do? "I felt the Jews were being destroyed," Schindler said later. "I had to help them. There was no choice."[33] Or as another rescuer explains, "One thing is important, I never made a moral decision to rescue Jews. I just got mad. I felt I had to do it. I came across many things that demanded my compassion." "I don't think that I did anything that special," says another. "What I did is what everybody normally should be doing. We all should help each other. It's common sense and common caring for people. We live in one world. We are one people. Working together, basically we are all the same."[34]

Such responses are fairly typical of rescuers who have been interviewed in recent studies, and support the claim that it was precisely this shared sense of humanity that moved them to action, rather than an abstract devotion to justice or the pursuit of a reflective moral principle. In her recent book *The Heart of Altruism*, Kristen Monroe describes dozens of conversations with rescuers such as those just quoted, and after considering all of the other approaches and explanations of "altruism," she finds that they are inadequate. She moves to this conclusion:

> It is this shared perception of themselves as part of an all-embracing humanity that was the one common characteristic that consistently and systematically distinguishes altruists from other individuals. It gives rise to an instinctive response that guides their actions in saving others and makes even life and death decisions nonconscious. Their perspective, their view of themselves as part of all humanity, constitutes such a central core to their identity that it leaves them the sense that they have no choice but to aid others in need.[35]

This is an important point, because it suggests that while in one sense the rescuers were "moral heroes," it is, in fact, more helpful to realize that their actions derived from a particular version of personal identity that emphasizes our ultimate belonging to each other and our relationship to humanity in general. In caring for those whom they rescued, Schindler, the Trocmés, and the others actively affirmed the reality of this view of things when it was most threatened by contemporary events. In their love of humanity, which was expressed through the care of their Jewish neighbors, they fulfilled this vision of the world and their participation in it.

Likewise, it is sometimes pointed out, as if it were a paradox, that in his own personal relationships and shady business dealings Oskar Schindler was hardly a "moral saint." The point, though, is that his decision to help the Jews did not so much derive from the desire for moral perfection as it did from the deeper sense of belonging to this greater community that affirms the absolute value of all of its members. To allow the Jews to die would be to repudiate that community, and so Schindler felt compelled to act.

At the very outset, I considered the possibility of a continuum of love in which from one perspective the love of humanity is love's fulfillment, while from a different perspective it is the most diluted form of love. Obviously, there are connections between the different kinds of love. There is compelling evidence to believe that the infant who does not receive love in his or her earliest years will be less able to form lasting friendships or romantic relationships when he or she is grown. One suspects that there must be some connection between the ability to care for specific friends and relatives and the ability to respond to a stranger when love and compassion are required, for all love involves an openness to the other and a willingness to focus on the latter in a caring way.

But while the various forms of love do support and enhance each other, there may also be situations in which the specific requirements of one kind of love may be at odds with those of another. As Tolstoy laments:

> In the name of what love are we to sacrifice another love? Whom shall we love more, to whom do more good,—to the wife or to the children, to the wife and to the children or to the friends? How are we to serve our beloved country, without impairing the love for wife, children, and friends? How, finally, am I to decide the question how much I may sacrifice of my personality which is needed in the service of others?[36]

Thus we may have to balance the competing claims of romance and friendship. In the case of rescuers, who sometimes endangered their own families by what they did, there is an obvious conflict between what the love of humanity required and what was required by the love of one's own spouse and children. In many cases, rescuers would be executed along with their whole family when they were caught. There is no easy way to settle these difficult moral conflicts, and this suggests that there is no final order of priority between the different kinds of love. One may be a very good parent who cares nothing about the plight of strangers. Or, like Schindler, one may be an erratic husband who is deeply devoted to others in need. There is a compelling argument in favor of the rescuer who knows she has to help even though this would endanger those she is closest to. But those who do not help out of concern for their families also have a moral point. Let us simply say that the different forms of love help to shape our sense of self in various ways. There is a very strong connection between personal identity and love; and through love, which involves an attunement to another person, we are able to gain the most profound awareness of who we are. The point is that we do not simply have a fixed and separate identity. In one regard, we may be human beings first of all and so share a common bond with everyone else. But one is also a friend, a child, a lover, a sibling, and a parent, and these aspects are equally important in determining who we are.

Finally, then, and to return to the love of humanity in light of all of this, we might ask *why* we find someone like Schindler or Schweitzer so admirable and worthy of emulation, even if we think that we would be unable to do as they did. In the case of Schindler, for instance, we must recognize his heroism and his courage given the obvious danger that he was in. Most people were afraid to help, but he went out of his way to protect hundreds of Jews, and he even rescued a whole trainload of people from Auschwitz. But there is something else that is involved in this case, and in less well-known examples of ordinary people who helped or saved people they did not know, even at considerable cost to themselves. First of all, we do not praise every act of self-sacrifice in the same way. A soldier may risk his own life for his comrade, which is an expression of the solidarity between them and against a common foe. Others may devote their lives to their families or to the poor, but if they do this at the obvious expense of their own individual development, we might not view their sacrifice as a sign of their own personal strength. The point is, we recognize the spirit in which the sacrifice is made. Similarly, in cases that involve self-mastery and self-assertion, we tend to respect someone who has recovered from incredible hardship or struggled against the odds to succeed, although we would not want to affirm the one who is devoted to self-aggrandizement at the expense of everyone else. By uniting these two kinds of examples, what seems to be *most* worthy and most admirable of all is an individual, like Schindler, who affirms both himself and others through his connection and involvement with them, even if he is threatened or about to be killed. In this case, therefore, we have a moral activity that is *also* a profound metaphysical affirmation: an example of self-assertion that is also a potential sacrifice and an affirmation of solidarity with others. In the end, the reason it appeals to us is because we know, at some level, that the model of human identity that it supports is actually the right one. As human beings, we are not solitary and isolated monads. We all belong to each other. We are all related to each other. And we are all responsible for each other. But this does not mean that we must cease to live our own lives or must deliberately relinquish our own specific goals. It simply means that we must love and care for our neighbor. In the love of humanity, which is expressed in the caring and compassionate involvement with another, a stranger, or simply one in need, we thereby confirm the ultimate solidarity of human existence that has just been described. And in striving to care for such an individual—whoever he or she may be—we are also affirming the value of every individual life, and the ultimate good of humanity itself.

I began this discussion of humanitarian love with the example of Albert Schweitzer, who gave up his own career in theology and music to minister to the sick in Africa. For Schweitzer, the decision to go to Lambarene was an act of love that followed from his profound commitment to the Christian religion. Over the years, however, Schweitzer came to appreciate the value of all life, for in opening himself to the needs of strangers and the plight of a suffering humanity, he could see no final distinction between human needs and the desire of all life to continue in being. Hence he came to his philosophy of "reverence for life." And while this may have been anticipated in the life of St. Francis, it goes beyond the norms of traditional Christianity. Schweitzer writes,

> As a being in active relation to the world, [man] comes into a spiritual relation with it by not living for himself alone, but by feeling himself with all life that comes within his reach. He will feel all that life's experiences as his own, he will give it all the help he possibly can, and will feel all the saving and promotion of life that he has been able to effect as the deepest happiness that can ever fall to his lot.
>
> Let a man once begin to think about the mystery of his life and the links which connect him with the life that fills the world, and he cannot but bring to bear upon his own life and all other life that comes within his reach the principle of Reverence for Life, and manifest this principle by ethical affirmation of life. Existence will thereby become harder for him in every respect than it would be if he lived for himself, but at the same time it will be richer, more beautiful and happier. It will become, instead of mere living, a real experience of life.[37]

Thus Schweitzer comes to essentially the same perspective as Buddha and Gandhi, who were very much aware of the suffering of all living creatures and refused to consider the sufferings of one as being any less important than those of another. In a sense, this is a mystical idea that arises from our everyday involvement with other creatures. It suggests that in the end love is the power that brings all things together and makes us aware of our mutual involvement and belonging to everything that is. Indeed, from this perspective, even the love of humanity would still be a limited kind of love.

Now we may or may not want to go as far as Schweitzer in affirming the universalist point of view. We might feel that he carries things to an impossible level when he worries over the flies in his operating room, or the germs that his medicines will destroy. Likewise, as a philosophical system, Schweitzer's account of "reverence for life" leaves much to be desired. But it is still important as an attempt to express a basic insight about our essential connectedness to all others and the respect in which every individual must be valued as unique and irreplaceable. Such an ethic of universal love is very appropriate for our own age, for we have largely lost a sense of the sacred, which this perspective evokes. At the same time, we are experiencing the questioning of all "essential" differences, such as masculine and feminine, rich or poor, or black and white, as well as the very idea of that which is "essentially human." The love of humanity cannot supersede the other kinds of love, which evoke other aspects of our personal identity, but the advent of a global community challenges the very provincial and provisional limitations of all our loving. At the very least, Schweitzer confirms the complete continuity of our love, for once we lovingly respond and open ourselves to another it does become much harder to close ourselves off to anyone else.

Thus, in the end, this reflection on the love of humanity leads us to something like a "religious" or metaphysical attitude toward the world: It is religious insofar as it leaves the limited perspective of the individual self and attempts to express our place in the overall scheme of things. And it is religious insofar as it affirms the ultimate value of human life and the human community, even though this cannot be supported or proved in any intellectual or "scientific" sense. This is an attitude that we are required to affirm even if we lack the moral courage to act. We recognize the "truth" of this attitude insofar as we respond to the compelling examples of those who have saved strangers or helped them even at great cost to themselves. This is the point of the Jewish Yad Vashem medal given to Holocaust rescuers, which says that "Whoever saves one life has saved humanity entire." In cases like these, the love of humanity that is expressed both affirms and evokes the ultimate value of human life and the sense in which we all belong to each other as a part of the greater community of women and men that cannot be denied.

Afterword

Philosophers have often been suspicious of love. Some have ignored it as philosophically irrelevant, while others have viewed love as dangerous because it undermines the rule of reason by encouraging our "lower" passionate selves. At first glance, Plato is an exception, for in the *Symposium* and in the *Phaedrus* he celebrates love as the power that first draws us out of ourselves and makes us yearn for that which is eternal and divine. But even in Plato, love is only the means to an end, with the final goal being the rapt contemplation of the Good. Thus Plato's ideal is Socrates, who has achieved self-sufficiency and who no longer needs love in the ordinary way, since to love would be an expression of his own inadequacy and need. At the outset of this work, I claimed that love involves a deep emotional commitment to another person. But at the same time, I argued that love is more than just an emotional experience, for it entails a responsiveness and an availability to the other person that means in some sense taking that person's interests and needs as if they were one's own. In Kantian language, love has both "practical" and "pathological" aspects that cannot be separated or denied: To love someone involves an emotional connectedness, but it also requires availability and a willingness to respond to the other person in an appropriate way. Likewise, I argued that loving someone involves the whole of one's being; through loving association with another, we may therefore experience moral, spiritual, *and* emotional fulfillment. Love is totally bound up with our sense of who we are. We come to know ourselves through love, and through this authentic association with another human being, we experience an enlargement of our own sense of self as the happiness and well-being of others becomes crucial to our own well-being. In this respect, it now seems obvious that the philosophical neglect of love has been a tremendous mistake.

The idea that there must be an inherent opposition between self-interest and the needs of the other is both a popular and a philosophical prejudice regarding love. But as we have seen, it is also misguided. When I love someone, I am at some level inspired with a sense of wonder by the mystery of the other person. However, this does not mean that in loving someone else I must be neglecting my own interests or even abandoning myself. In the *Symposium*, Plato seems to think that once Socrates has achieved the "ultimate" standpoint, any profound association with others—such as Alcibiades—can only bring him down again. And in the *Confessions*, St. Augustine, like many other early Christians, warns against excessive attachments to other people because these will lure us away from the most important relationship to God. Now, when I love someone else I am really opening myself to that person in the fullest possible way, accepting who he or she is and encouraging and allowing the beloved to be himself or herself. But through this most authentic encounter with another person I am also inspired and will experience a moral, spiritual, and emotional transformation that will often evoke the very best aspects of who I am. In this way, self-understanding and awareness of the other are intimately connected. Without the beloved I would remain fixed and self-contained, and I would never know the enlargement of spirit that the experience of love involves. Plato understood at least this much when he made love of particular beauty the first step toward the ultimate apprehension of the Good. Love is, therefore, the key to my own sense of self and my own well-being, and the false but familiar opposition between self and other finally breaks down at this point.

In this book, I have considered what I take to be the four most basic expressions of love—romantic love, friendship, parental love, and the love of humanity—and I have tried to show how each particular kind of love expresses a different aspect or modality of self-fulfillment and our authentic being with others. Thus, friendship is an inherently moral phenomenon that encourages our own moral growth. The love of humanity allows us to experience a sense of belonging to, and to affirm our deep metaphysical connection with, all human beings. Romantic love offers the most intense possibilities of emotional, spiritual, and physical fulfillment, while it breaks down the boundaries between these different domains. Parental love emphasizes caring and nurturing and allows us to participate in the pure generosity of life. Obviously, the different kinds of love will often overlap with each other, for friendship involves elements of caring and nurturing, and romantic love and the love of humanity are not unrelated in the possibilities of moral enhancement and growth. But I think that the perspective I have chosen in each case brings out the most essential features of the different kinds of love and helps us to see why they have typically been distinguished from each other.

This survey of the different kinds of love is complete now, for it may be argued that every particular experience of love involves some reference to these four most basic types. The religious love of God, for instance, may follow the model of humanitarian love, or even romantic love in the case of the saint who yearns desperately for the divine. The love of animals is very closely related to the kind of caring that is involved in parental love, and perhaps also to the friendship that exists between two beings who know and value each other. The love of children for their parents may actually be the first model for romantic love, if the parent is exalted as the "one and only," or this relationship may be closer to friendship, especially if it involves adult children and their parents. There is no order or hierarchy between the different kinds of love, and since they are the most basic types of love, it is not the case that any one of them can be deduced from any of the others. Each makes its appeal to a separate but related aspect of who we are; all together, they allow us to flourish as human beings. In the final analysis, love takes us out of our isolation, and at the same time that it clarifies and enlarges our sense of who we are, it also creates our most authentic community with other people.

Throughout this work, I have focused attention on the history of love's different determinations and on the fact, which is often ignored, that friendship, parental love, romantic love, and the love of humanity all have a particular historical formation. In this way it is possible to gain more of a critical distance from the current received ideas about love, which should be critically considered. There are many myths about love and many fixed ideas about friendship, parental love, altruistic love, or romance that may not be valid or always appropriate or even in the spirit of love itself. Thus, I have not tried to offer a final definition of love or a theory of what love is. Love is complex and overdetermined, and to understand it completely one would have to understand the complex history of its various manifestations or the genealogy of its particular forms. Using this approach, commonalities do emerge between the ancient Greek and contemporary accounts of friendship, for example, or between modern romantic love and its courtly antecedent. And through comparison we can also glimpse an ideal—not the pure "Form" of friendship, romantic love, parental love, or altruism, but a vision of each of these different kinds of love that is relevant to us and worth striving for insofar as it would promote an even deeper connection to others and the fulfillment of oneself. As for the commonalities that might emerge at the level of "love in general," we should remember that every manifestation of love is a particular manifestation of romantic love, friendship, altruism, or caring, and beyond this there is no experience of "love in itself" that is unconnected to a particular object or a particular context. Nevertheless, I have argued throughout this book that all of the different expressions of love share emotional cherishing and availability and project the possibility of self-fulfillment through a more or less intense and complete encounter with another person. In the sense that it is possible to talk about such things, it would be true to say that something like this is really the implicit end or the goal of "love in general," and this allows us to examine all of the popular and philosophical ideas about love to determine whether they are adequate to this ideal.

Finally, much of the discussion in this book has concerned the future of love and the role that various kinds of love might have in a future (or a better) society. By looking at the past and present realities of love in its different manifestations, I have tried to illustrate the future possibilities of loving that might be available to us in times to come. It is sometimes argued, for example, that we now live in a world that is increasingly dehumanized and subject to technological order and control. And in this so-called postmodern age, human relationships, like everything else, are becoming commodified and reduced to their basic instrumental value. Likewise, today the traditional models of love are often viewed ironically as interesting possibilities of experience or are dismissed as relics of a bygone age that we can now dispense with. This means that the models of love that we have lived by can no longer be taken for granted. We probably are at a point of transition when love, along with every other ideological form, must be critically scrutinized to see whether it measures up to its own inherent ideal. For the most part in history, it is difficult to step back from all of one's received ideas and beliefs about the world because as long as these are in the ascendant they seem like the natural and inevitable features of all human experience, and we have no other models for thinking about our lives. In a time of transition, however, the ruling ideas loosen their hold on us, and the prevailing models begin to seem more problematic. At this point, we have a much better chance to think for ourselves—and so we can consider the genuine possibilities of love that might become available to us, and we can reject the inadequate models of friendship, romantic love and so forth that have prevailed so far.

In short, we need to reflect upon "love's philosophy," and although this is always difficult, we are now living in an age when this may actually be easier than it has been in the past. As I have tried to show in this book, our reflection must include conceptual and philosophical analysis, but it must also involve an inquiry into history, psychology, literature, and other perspectives of human experience. There is no a priori truth about love, but neither is the truth of love only a generalization from human experience so far. In this book I have argued that the basic varieties of love are vitally important as ways of self-recollection that would otherwise be unavailable to us, while at the same time they project the possibilities of an authentic encounter with another person and with human beings in general. In this sense, love is one of the most crucial things that defines us as human in the first place. Certainly, we could still exist without it, but without it we would not be human in the same significant sense.

Notes

Introduction

1. Leo Tolstoy, *Anna Karenina*, trans. Constance Garnett (New York: Random House, 1965), p. 421.

2. Immanuel Kant, *The Fundamental Principles of the Metaphysics of Morals*, trans. Herbert J. Paton, in *The Moral Law* (London: Hutchinson, 1976), p. 65 (399).

3. Plato, *Symposium*, trans. Micheal Joyce, in *The Collected Dialogues of Plato*, ed. Edith Hamilton and Huntington Cairns (Princeton, N.J.: Princeton University Press, 1978), p. 563 (211d).

Chapter 1: Friendship and the Good

1. See Cicero, "On Friendship," trans. Frank. Copley, in *Other Selves: Philosophers on Friendship*, ed. Michael Pakaluk (Indianapolis, Ind.: Hackett, 1991), p. 85. For the original attribution of this quotation to Aristotle, see Diogenes Laertius, *Lives of Eminent Philosophers*, vol. 1, trans. Robert D. Hicks (Cambridge, Mass.: Harvard University Press, 1959) at V 21.

2. See John Huizinga, *The Waning of the Middle Ages* (New York: Anchor Books, 1954) for a discussion of this distinction in the context of the courtly ideals of love.

3. Aristotle, *Nicomachean Ethics*, trans. Terence Irwin, in Pakaluk, *Other Selves*, 1171b. All future citations from Aristotle refer to this edition.

4. See Seneca, "On Philosophy and Friendship," Epistle IX, trans. Richard M. Gummere in Pakaluk, *Other Selves*.

5. See Aristotle, *Nichomachean Ethics*, p. 56 (1166a): "The decent person, then, has each of these features in relation to himself, and is related to his friend as he is to himself, since the friend is another himself." Also see p. 65 (1170b): "The excellent person is related to his friend in the same way as he is related to himself, since a friend is another himself."

6. Cicero, "On Friendship," p. 88.

7. See Charles Kahn, "Aristotle and Altruism," *Mind* 90 (1981): 20–40.

8. See Kahn, "Aristotle and Altruism" and also Suzanne Stern-Gillett, *Aristotle's Theory of Friendship* (Albany: State University of New York Press, 1985).

9. Kahn, "Aristotle and Altruism," p. 38.

10. See Aristotle, *Nichomachean Ethics*, 1159a–1161b.

11. Here I have benefited considerably from discussions in Lawrence Blum, *Friendship, Altruism and Morality* (London: Routledge, 1980) and also Lawrence Thomas, "Friendship and Other Loves," in *Friendship: A Philosophical Reader*, ed. Neera K. Badhwar (Ithaca, N.Y.: Cornell University Press, 1993), p. 48–64.

12. Alasdair MacIntyre, *After Virtue* (Notre Dame, Ind.: University of Notre Dame Press), p. 156.

13. See, for example, Marilyn Friedman, *What Are Friends For: Feminist Perspectives on Personal Relationships and Moral Theory* (Ithaca, N.Y.: Cornell University Press, 1993) and Janet Raymond, *A Passion for Friends* (Boston: Beacon Press, 1986).

14. C. S. Lewis, *Four Talks on Love* (Atlanta: The Parish of the Air, n.d.), audio-cassette. These talks are an earlier version of *The Four Loves* (New York: Harcourt, Brace, Jovanovich, 1960).

15. Lewis, *Four Loves*, p. 102.

16. Lillian Rubin, *Just Friends* (New York: Harper and Row, 1985), and Letty Pogrebin, *Among Friends* (New York: McGraw-Hill, 1987).

17. Rubin, *Just Friends*, p. 60.

18. Ibid., p. 63.

19. Montaigne, "Of Friendship," trans. Donald Frame, in Pakaluk, *Other Selves*, pp. 190–191.

20. Cicero, *De Amicitia*, xi. 37, trans. Frank Copley, in Pakaluk, *Other Selves*, pp. 93–94.

21. Seneca, "On Philosophy and Friendship," Epistle IX, trans. Richard M. Gummere, in Pakaluk *Other Selves*, p. 121.

22. See Friedman, *What Are Friends For*, chapter 7, "Friendship and Moral Growth," pp. 187–206. See also Paul Wadell, *Friendship and the Moral Life* (Notre Dame, Ind.: University of Notre Dame Press, 1989).

23. Cited by Cyril Connolly in "The Unquiet Grave," in *The Oxford Book of Friendship*, ed. D. J. Enright and David Rawlinson (Oxford: Oxford University Press, 1992), p. 19.

24. Charles Dickens, *David Copperfield* (Oxford: Oxford University Press, 1987), p. 455.

25. Lewis, *Four Loves*, p. 88.

26. See Friedman, *What Are Friends For*, especially her chapter on "Feminism and Modern Friendship," pp. 231–255; also see Rubin, *Just Friends*, pp. 170–174.

27. Montaigne, "Of Friendship," p. 192.

Chapter 2: The Value of Romantic Love

1. Johann Wolfgang von Goethe, *The Sorrows of Young Werther*, trans. Elizabeth Mayer and Louise Bogan (New York: Random House, 1990), p. 69.

2. For an important defense of romantic love and its possibilities for personal fulfillment, see Robert Solomon, "The Virtue of (Erotic) Love," in *The Philosophy of (Erotic) Love*, ed. Robert Solomon and Kathleen Higgins (Lawrence: University of Kansas Press), pp. 492–518.

3. See Stendhal, *On Love*, trans. Gilbert Sale and Suzanne Sale (Harmondsworth: Penguin, 1977).

4. William Hazlitt, *Liber Amoris* (Oxford: Woodstock Books, 1992), p. 27.

5. Goethe, *Werther*, p. 47.

6. On this point, see Roger Scruton's discussion in *Sexual Desire* (New York: Macmillan, 1986), pp. 213–252.

7. Romans 7:21–23 (New English Bible).

8. Thomas Mann, *Death in Venice,* in *Death in Venice and Seven Other Stories,* trans. H. T. Lowe-Porter (New York: Random House, 1963), p. 25.

9. Stendhal, *On Love,* pp. 285–286.

10. Ibid., p. 60.

11. Plato, *Phaedrus,* in *The Collected Dialogues of Plato,* ed. Edith Hamilton and Huntington Cairns (Princeton, N.J.: Princeton University Press, 1960), p. 501 (255e).

12. Hazlitt, *Liber Amoris,* p. 65.

13. Stendhal, *On Love,* p. 114.

14. Goethe, *Werther,* p. 111.

15. Plato, *Symposium,* trans. Alexander Nehamas and Paul Woodruff (Indianapolis, Ind.: Hackett, 1989), p. 29 (192e).

16. Shelley, "Epipsychidion," in *The Complete Poems of Keats and Shelley* (New York: Routledge, n.d.), p. 477, lines 565–587.

17. D. H. Lawrence, *Women in Love* (New York: Barnes and Noble, 1996), p. 354.

18. Ibid., p. 239.

19. Goethe, *Werther,* p. 138.

20. Ibid., p. 157.

21. Ibid., p. 102, 117.

22. Shulamith Firestone, *The Dialectic of Sex: The Case for Feminist Revolution* (New York: Bantam, 1970), pp. 146–147.

23. Simone de Beauvoir, *The Second Sex,* trans. H. M. Parshley (Harmondsworth: Penguin, 1981), p. 653.

24. Virginia Woolf, *To the Lighthouse* (New York: Harcourt, Brace, Jovanovich, 1955), p. 150.

25. Emily Brontë, *Wuthering Heights* (Ware: Wordsworth Press, 1996), pp. 99–100.

26. Rainer Maria Rilke, *Letters to a Young Poet,* trans. Stephen Mitchell (New York: Random House, 1984), p. 55.

27. Luce Irigaray has offered some very powerful feminist readings of classic philosophical texts. She has also written extensively from a psychoanalytical perspective. In other texts, including *Elemental Passions,* trans. Joanne Collie and Judith Still (New York: Routledge, 1992), she has tried a more provocative, poetic, and feminine style of writing that seeks to avoid the traditional presuppositions of (male) philosophical discourse.

28. Irigaray, *Elemental Passions,* p. 27.

29. Ibid., p. 15.

30. Ibid., p. 16.

31. Ibid., p. 28.

32. Luce Irigaray, *I Love to You,* trans. Alison Martin (New York: Routledge, 1996), p. 24.

33. Woolf, *To the Lighthouse,* p. 155.

34. de Beauvoir, *Second Sex,* pp. 677–679.

35. Compare Christopher Lasch, *The Culture of Narcissism* (New York: Norton, 1991). In this book, Lasch argues that narcissism is the dominant trope of contemporary experience.

Chapter 3: From Parents to Children

1. Philippe Aries, *Centuries of Childhood*, trans. Robert Baldick (New York: Knopf, 1962), p. 128.

2. St. Augustine, *Confessions*, trans. R. S. Pine-Coffin (Harmondsworth: Penguin, 1974), p. 27.

3. Edmund Gosse, *Father and Son* (Boston: Houghton Mifflin, 1965).

4. For a good discussion of the difference between maternal and paternal love as commonly conceived, see Erich Fromm, *The Art of Loving* (London: Allen and Unwin, 1969), pp. 35–38.

5. The example is from Nel Noddings, *Caring* (Berkeley: University of California Press, 1984), p. 44.

6. Adrienne Rich, *Of Woman Born: Motherhood as Experience and Institution* (New York: Norton, 1986), p. 52.

7. Elizabeth Badinter, *Mother Love*, trans. Francine du Plessisc Gray. (New York: Macmillan, 1981), p. xix.

8. From Montaigne's *Essays*, bk. 2, ch. 8. Quoted by Badinter, *Mother Love*, p. 62.

9. Charles Dickens, *Hard Times* (New York: New American Library, 1980), p. 12.

10. Ibid., p. 29.

11. Ibid., p. 102.

12. Ibid., p. 105.

13. Ibid., p. 215.

14. On this point, see the essay by Frank R. Leavis, "*Hard Times*: The World of Bentham," in his *The World of Dickens* (London: Chatto, 1970), pp. 187–212.

15. Honoré de Balzac, *Pere Goriot*, trans. Henry Reed. (New York: Signet, 1962), p. 93.

16. Ibid., p. 255.

17. Ibid., p. 118.

18. Ibid., p. 205.

19. Toni Morrison, *Beloved* (New York: Penguin, 1987), p. 163.

20. Ibid., p. 16.

21. Ibid., p. 203.

22. Rich, *Of Woman Born*, p. 13.

23. Shulamith Firestone, *The Dialectic of Sex: The Case for Feminist Revolution* (New York: Bantam, 1970), p. 104.

24. Plato, *Symposium*, in *The Collected Dialogues of Plato*, ed. Edith Hamilton and Huntington Cairns (Princeton, N.J.: Princeton University Press, 1960), p. 560 (208a).

25. Freud, "On Narcissism," in *The Complete Works of Sigmund Freud*, vol. 14, ed. James Strachey (London: Hogarth Press, 1973), p. 90.

26. Ibid., p. 91.

27. Sara Ruddick, *Maternal Thinking* (New York: Ballantine, 1990), p. 121.

28. Noddings, *Caring*, p. 193.

29. Ibid., p. 126.

30. Plato, *The Republic*, in *Collected Dialogues*, p. 696 (457d).

31. Ibid., p. 126.

32. See Jean-Jacques Rousseau, *The Social Contract*, in *Basic Political Writings of Jean-Jacques Rousseau*, trans. and ed. Donald A. Cress (Indianapolis, Ind.: Hackett, 1987), especially pp. 155–156 on the difference between the general will and the will of all (bk. 2, ch. 31).

33. Charlotte P. Gilman, *Herland* (New York: Random House, 1979), p. 95.

34. Ibid., p. 66.

Chapter 4: For the Love of Humanity

1. An essential aspect of Stoic ethics was to be of service to all human beings, regardless of laws, conventions, or property, since all human beings, as rational creatures, were supposed to possess the same creative fire.

2. See Mo Tzu, "Universal Love," in *Basic Writings of Mo Tzu, Hsün Tzu and Han Fei Tzu*, trans. Burton Watson (New York: Columbia University Press, 1967), pp. 39–49.

3. John 14:34 (Revised Standard Version).

4. Sigmund Freud, *Civilization and its Discontents*, trans. James Strachey (New York: Norton, 1961), p. 56.

5. Ibid., p. 57.

6. St. Augustine, *Confessions*, trans. R. S. Pine-Coffin (Harmondsworth: Penguin, 1989), p. 79.

7. Søren Kierkegaard, "You Shall Love Your Neighbour" (from *Works of Love*), in *Other Selves: Philosophers on Friendship*, ed. Michael Pakaluk (Indianapolis, Ind.: Hackett, 1991), pp. 235–247.

8. Sigmund Freud, "On Narcissism," in *The Complete Works of Sigmund Freud*, vol. 14, ed. James Strachey (London: Hogarth Press, 1973), p. 91.

9. Ibid., p. 88.

10. Freud, *Civilization and Its Discontents*, p. 96.

11. Ibid., p. 33.

12. Ibid., p. 81.

13. Ibid., p. 66.

14. From Shelley, "Epipsychidion," in *The Complete Poems of Keats and Shelley* (New York: Routledge, n.d.), line 161.

15. See, for example, Frederich Nietzsche, "On Love of the Neighbour," in *Thus Spoke Zarathustra*, trans. Walter Kaufmann, in *The Portable Nietzsche* (London: Chatto, 1971), pp. 172–174.

16. Max Scheler, *Ressentiment*, trans. William W. Holdheim (New York: Schocken, 1972), p. 95.

17. See David Hume, *An Inquiry Concerning the Principles of Morals* (Indianapolis, Ind.: Bobbs-Merrill, 1957), especially "On Benevolence," pp. 9–14.

18. Luke 10:30–35.

19. Testimony of Moshe Bejhki in the documentary film *Schindler*, by John Blair (Thames, 1980).

20. Most influential here is Anders Nygren, *Agape and Eros*, trans. Philip S. Watson (New York: Harper, 1953).

21. Plato, *Symposium*, trans. Alexander Nehamas and Paul Woodruff (Indianapolis, Ind.: Hackett, 1989), p. 59 (211e).

22. Ibid., p. 70 (218e).

23. John 15:12.

24. 1 John 4:7.

25. 1 John 4:12.

26. Mark 11:30–31.

27. See Luke 15:11–32.

28. C. S. Lewis, *Four Talks on Love* (Atlanta: The Parish of the Air, n.d.), audiocassette. These talks are an earlier version of *The Four Loves* (New York: Harcourt, Brace, Jovanovich, 1960).

29. Nygren, *Agape and Eros,* p. 34.

30. See Nygren, *Agape and Eros,* pp. 75–81.

31. For further discussion of this theme, see Janet Soskice, "Love and Attention," in *Philosophy, Religion and the Spiritual Life,* ed. Michael McGhee (New York: Cambridge University Press, 1992).

32. For further discussion of these issues, see the collection *Altruism,* ed. Ellen Frankel Paul, Fred D. Miller Jr., and Jeffrey Paul. (New York: Cambridge University Press, 1993).

33. *Schindler.*

34. These comments and many others are included in Kristen Monroe, *The Heart of Altruism* (Princeton, N.J.: Princeton University Press, 1996).

35. Ibid., p. 213.

36. Leo Tolstoy, *Collected Works,* vol. 16, "On Life," trans. and ed. Leo Wiener (New York: Colonial Press), p. 330.

37. Albert Schweitzer, *Out of My Life and Thought,* trans. Charles T. Campion (New York: Holt, 1957), p. 231.

Bibliography

General Works on Love

Bergmann, Martin. *The Anatomy of Loving*. New York: Columbia University Press, 1987.

Bloom, Allan. *Love and Friendship*. New York: Simon and Schuster, 1993.

Dilman, Ilham. *Love and Human Separateness*. Oxford: Basil Blackwell, 1987.

Fromm, Erich. *The Art of Loving*. New York: Bantam, 1956.

Goicoechea, David, ed. *The Nature and Pursuit of Love*. Buffalo, N.Y.: Prometheus Books, 1995.

Kristeva, Julia. *Tales of Love*. New York: Columbia University Press, 1987.

Lewis, C. S. *The Four Loves*. New York: Harcourt Brace Jovanovich, 1960.

Norton, David L., and Mary F. Kille, eds. *Philosophies of Love*. San Francisco: Chandler, 1971.

Nussbaum, Martha C. *Love's Knowledge: Essays in Philosophy and Literature*. Oxford: Oxford University Press, 1990.

Ortega y Gasset, José. *On Love*. Translated by Toby Talbot. New York: Meridian, 1957.

Singer, Irving. *The Nature of Love*. 3 vols. Chicago: University of Chicago Press, 1966–1987.

———. *The Pursuit of Love*. Baltimore: Johns Hopkins University Press, 1995.

Soble, Alan. *The Structure of Love*. New Haven: Yale University Press, 1990.

———, ed. *Eros, Agape, and Philia: Readings in the Philosophy of Love*. New York: Paragon House, 1989.

Solomon, Robert. *About Love*. New York: Simon and Schuster, 1988.

———. *Love: Emotion, Myth and Metaphor*. Buffalo, N.Y.: Prometheus Books, 1990.

Solomon, Robert, and Kathleen Higgins. *The Philosophy of (Erotic) Love*. Lawrence: University of Kansas Press, 1991.

Stewart, Robert. *Philosophical Perspectives on Sex and Love*. Oxford: Oxford University Press, 1995.

Williams, Clifford, ed. *On Love and Friendship*. Boston: Jones and Bartlett, 1995.

Friendship

Annas, Julia. "Plato and Aristotle on Friendship and Altruism." *Mind* 86 (1977): 532–554.

Annis, David. "Emotion, Love and Friendship." *International Journal of Applied Philosophy* 4 (1988): 1–7.

Armstrong, Robert L. "Friendship." *Journal of Value Inquiry* 19 (1985): 211–216.

Badhwar, Neera Kapur. "Friendship, Justice and Supererogation." *American Philosophical Quarterly* 22 (1985): 123–131.

———, ed. *Friendship: A Philosophical Reader*. Ithaca, N.Y.: Cornell University Press, 1992.

Blum, Lawrence. *Friendship, Altruism and Morality*. London: Routledge and Kegan Paul, 1980.

Dickens, Charles. *David Copperfield*. Oxford: Oxford University Press, 1987.

Enright, D. J., and David Rawlinson, eds. *Oxford Book of Friendship*. Oxford: Oxford University Press, 1991.

Friedman, Marilyn. *What Are Friends For: Feminist Perspectives on Personal Relationships and Moral Theory*. Ithaca, N.Y.: Cornell University Press, 1993.

Gilbert, Paul. "Friendship and the Will." *Philosophy* 61 (1986): 61–70.

Kahn, Charles. "Aristotle and Altruism." *Mind* 90 (1981): 20–40.

MacIntyre, Alasdair. *After Virtue*. Notre Dame, Ind.: University of Notre Dame Press, 1984.

Morrison, Toni. *Sula*. New York: Knopf, 1973.

Pakaluk, Michael, ed. *Other Selves: Philosophers on Friendship*. Indianapolis, Ind.: Hackett, 1991.

Pogrebin, Letty. *Among Friends*. New York: McGraw-Hill, 1987.

Price, A. W. *Love and Friendship in Plato and Aristotle*. Oxford: Clarendon Press, 1989.

Raymond, Janet. *A Passion for Friends*. Boston: Beacon Press, 1986.

Rubin, Lillian. *Just Friends: The Role of Friendship in Our Lives*. New York: Harper and Row, 1985.

Stern-Gillett, Suzanne. *Aristotle's Theory of Friendship*. Albany: State University of New York Press, 1985.

Wadell, Paul. *Friendship and the Moral Life*. Notre Dame, Ind.: University of Notre Dame Press, 1989.

Romantic Love

Barthes, Roland. *A Lover's Discourse*. Translated by Richard Howard. New York: Hill and Wang, 1978.

de Beauvoir, Simone. *The Second Sex*. Translated by H. M. Parshley. Harmondsworth: Penguin, 1981.

Benjamin, Jessica. "The Bonds of Love: Rational Violence and Erotic Domination." *Feminist Studies* 6 (1980): 144–174.

Berenson, Frances. "What Is This Thing Called Love?" *Philosophy* 66 (1991): 65–79.

Brontë, Emily. *Wuthering Heights*. Ware: Wordsworth Press, 1996.

Caraway, Carol. "Romantic Love—Neither Sexist nor Heterosexist." *Philosophy and Theology* 1 (1987): 361–368.

———. "Romantic Love: A Patchwork." *Philosophy and Theology* 2 (1987): 76–96.

Firestone, Shulamith. *The Dialectic of Sex: The Case for Feminist Revolution*. New York: William Morrow, 1970.

Gaylin, Willard, and Ethel Person, eds. *Passionate Attachments: Thinking about Love*. New York: Free Press, 1988.

Giddens, Anthony. *The Transformation of Intimacy*. Stanford: Stanford University Press, 1992.

Goethe, Johann Wolfgang von. *The Sorrows of Young Werther*. Translated by Elizabeth Mayer and Louise Bogan. New York: Random House, 1990.

Gregory, Paul. "Eroticism and Love." *American Philosophical Quarterly* 25 (1988): 339–344.

———. "The Two Sides of Love." *Journal of Applied Philosophy* 3 (1986): 229–233.

Hazlitt, William. *Liber Amoris*. Oxford: Woodstock Books, 1992.

Hunt, Morton. *The Natural History of Love*. New York: Barnes and Noble, 1993.

Irigaray, Luce. *Elemental Passions*. Translated by Joanne Collie and Judith Still. New York: Routledge, 1992.

———. *An Ethics of Sexual Difference*. Translated by Gillian Gill and Carolyn Burke. Ithaca, N.Y.: Cornell University Press, 1993.

———. *I Love to You*. Translated by Alison Martin. London: Routledge, 1996.

———. "Sorcerer Love." *Hypatia* 3 (1989): 32–44.

Lamb, Roger, ed. *Love Analyzed*. Boulder, Colo.: Westview Press, 1997.

Lasch, Christopher. *The Culture of Narcissism*. New York: Norton, 1991.

Lawrence, D. H. *Women in Love*. New York: Barnes and Noble, 1996.

Letwin, Shirley Robin. "Romantic Love and Christianity." *Philosophy* 52 (1977): 131–145.

Mann, Thomas. *Death in Venice and Seven Other Stories*. Translated by H. T. Lowe-Porter. New York: Random House, 1963.

Nye, Andrea. "The Subject of Love." *Journal of Value Inquiry* 24 (1990): 135–153.

Person, Ethel. *Dreams of Love and Fateful Encounters*. New York: Penguin, 1989.

Pintar, Judith. *The Halved Soul: Retelling the Myths of Romantic Love*. London: HarperCollins, 1992.

Plato, *Phaedrus*. Translated by Reginald Hackforth.. In *The Collected Dialogues of Plato*. Edited by Edith Hamilton and Huntington Cairns. Princeton: Princeton University Press, 1960.

Plato, *Symposium*. Translated by Michael Joyce. In *The Collected Dialogues of Plato*. Edited by Edith Hamilton and Huntington Cairns. Princeton: Princeton University Press, 1960.

Plato, *Symposium*. Translated by Alexander Nehamas and Paul Woodruff. Indianapolis, Ind.: Hackett, 1989.

Rilke, Rainer Maria. *Letters to a Young Poet*. Translated by Stephen Mitchell. New York: Random House, 1984.

———. *Rilke on Love and Other Difficulties*. New York: Norton, 1975.

de Rougemont, Denis. *Love in the Western World*. Translated by Montgomery Belgion. New York: Schocken Books, 1990.

Scruton, Roger. *Sexual Desire*. New York: Macmillan, 1986.

Shelley, Percy Bysshe. "Epipsychidion." In *The Complete Poems of Keats and Shelley*. New York: Routledge, n.d.

Soble, Alan. "The Unity of Romantic Love." *Philosophy and Theology* 1 (1987): 374–397.

Solomon, Robert. "The Virtue of Love." *Midwest Studies in Philosophy* 13 (1988): 12–31.

Stendhal, Henri. *On Love*. Translated by Gilbert Sale and Suzanne Sale. Harmondsworth: Penguin, 1977.

Tolstoy, Leo. *Anna Karenina*. Translated by Constance Garnett. New York: Random House, 1965.

Vlastos, Gregory. "The Individual as an Object of Love in Plato." In *Platonic Studies*. Princeton, N.J.: Princeton University Press, 1973.

Warner, Martin. "Love, Self, and Plato's Symposium." *Philosophical Quarterly* 29 (1979): 329–339.

Woolf, Virginia. *To the Lighthouse.* New York: Harcourt Brace Jovanovich, 1955.

Parental Love

Archard, David. *Children: Rights and Childhood.* London: Routledge, 1993.

Aries, Philippe. *Centuries of Childhood.* Translated by Robert Baldick. New York: Knopf, 1962.

Augustine, Saint. *Confessions.* Translated by R. S. Pine-Coffin. Harmondsworth: Penguin, 1974.

Badinter, Elizabeth. *Mother Love.* Translated by Francine du Plessis Gray. New York: Macmillan, 1981.

Balzac, Honoré de. *Pere Goriot.* Translated by Henry Reed. New York: Signet, 1962.

Dickens, Charles. *Hard Times.* New York: Signet, 1980.

Emecheta, Buchi. *The Joys of Motherhood.* New York: George Braziller, 1979.

Freud, Sigmund. "On Narcissism." In *The Complete Works of Sigmund Freud.* Vol. 14. Translated and edited by James Strachey. London: Hogarth Press, 1973.

Gilman, Charlotte P. *Herland.* New York: Random House, 1979.

Gosse, Edmund. *Father and Son.* Boston: Houghton Mifflin, 1965.

Hwang, C. Philip, Michael Lamb, and Irving Sigel, eds. *Images of Childhood.* New Jersey: Lawrence Erlbaum Associates, 1996.

Kupfer, Joseph. "Can Parents and Children Be Friends?" *American Philosophical Quarterly* 27 (1990): 15–26.

Morrison, Toni. *Beloved.* New York: Penguin, 1988.

Noddings, Nel. *Caring.* Berkeley: University of California, 1984.

Plato. *Republic.* In *Collected Dialogues of Plato.* Edited by Edith Hamilton and Huntington Cairns. Princeton, N.J.: Princeton University Press, 1960.

Rich, Adrienne. *Of Woman Born: Motherhood as Experience and Institution.* New York: Norton, 1988.

Ruddick, Sara. *Maternal Thinking.* New York: Ballantine, 1990.

Sommerville, John. *The Rise and Fall of Childhood.* Beverly Hills, Calif.: Sage Publications, 1982.

The Love of Humanity

Brümmer, Vincent. *The Model of Love.* Cambridge: Cambridge University Press, 1993.

Freud, Sigmund. *Civilization and Its Discontents.* Translated by James Strachey. New York: Norton, 1961.

Hume, David. *An Inquiry Concerning the Principles of Morals.* Indianapolis, Ind.: Bobbs-Merrill, 1975.

Monroe, Kristen. *The Heart of Altruism.* Princeton, N.J.: Princeton University Press, 1976.

Nietzsche, Frederick. *Thus Spoke Zarathustra.* Translated by Walter Kaufmann. In *The Portable Nietzsche.* London: Chatto, 1971.

Nygren, Anders. *Agape and Eros.* Translated by Philip S. Watson. New York: Harper, 1953.

Outka, Gene. *Agape: An Ethical Analysis.* New Haven, Conn.: Yale University Press, 1972.

Paul, Ellen Frankel, Fred D. Miller Jr., and Jeffrey Paul, eds. *Altruism*. New York: Cambridge University Press, 1993.

Scheler, Max. *Ressentiment*. Translated by William W. Holdheim. New York: Schocken, 1972.

Schweitzer, Albert. *Out of My Life and Thought*. Translated by Charles T. Campion. New York: Holt, 1957.

Soskice, Janet. "Love and Attention." In *Philosophy, Religion and the Spiritual Life*. Edited by Michael McGhee. New York: Cambridge University Press, 1992.

Tzu, Mo. "Universal Love." In *Basic Writings of Mo Tzu, Hsün Tzu and Han Fei Tzu*. Translated by Burton Watson. New York: Columbia University Press, 1967.

Vacek, Edward. *Love, Human and Divine: The Heart of Christian Ethics*. Washington, D.C.: Georgetown University Press, 1974.

Index

About the Author

Richard White is an associate professor of philosophy at Creighton University, Omaha. He is the author of *Nietzsche and the Problem of Sovereignty* (Illinois) and the editor of *Critical and Historical Perspectives in Philosophy: Nietzsche* (Ashgate).